doorw

meditations on Ps

by John Scarland

doorway
meditations on Psalm 119
by John Scarland

ISBN: 9781973166375
Imprint: Independently published

Foreword

Very favourite books can be read many times over; the written words come alive and you are enthused to revisit familiar places and amazed to discover new places. It has been my privilege to not only read Doorway but to listen to each module as, over the past year, John has explained and illustrated the meaning of Psalm 119 at our Church services. I have at various times been challenged, encouraged, rebuked and soothed as I have heard the spoken word, but reading the written word has intensified the reality of my relationship with God as the words are absorbed into my mind and my being.

I have known John and Ruth for many years and John doesn't follow tradition! The truths of the Bible are very much part of who John is, yet there is a sense of discovery and freshness to Doorway as John marvels once again at God's steadfast love for him and for us – God's creation who have got things so wrong and would continue to get things wrong without the roadmap in Psalm 119.

What did I know about Psalm 119 before I set out on this journey. I knew it was the longest Psalm in the Bible and maybe one or two "go to" verses, but not how it reflects the depth of God's constant love and care for one who constantly needs to be reminded. Doorway is so many things – see how the illustrations visualise the content of each module and lead you along the path of life; maybe read a page or chapter each morning, or evening, and let the words draw you near to God for the help and wisdom we need in our daily Christian life. Or read the book as a whole and observe the progression and contemplate how the issues we face today are not dissimilar from those faced by the Psalmist who shows us the right way forward from his own experience and, even more, the guide that accompanied the Psalmist is absolutely the same guide who walks with us.

The Psalmist was on a journey with God and so are we. Make sure you keep Doorway and the words of Psalm 119 close by.

Jennifer Smith
January 2018

thanks

thanks to Jennifer Smith, a long term
friend whose agreement to help
gave me the confidence to begin the
doorway project
Her extensive work on my ramshackle
manuscript was crucial to the
publishing of this book

and thanks to my wife Ruth for all her
loving and giving over so many years
that has underpinned our life and
service for the Lord

first look at 119

this Psalm or poem is a careful construction
and quite quickly we notice it follows a distinct pattern

the whole Psalm is made up of 22 modules,
each module is attached to one of the 22 letters in the Hebrew alphabet.
all the modules have eight couplets, each beginning with its own Hebrew letter,
Aleph, Beth, Gimel etc
and each couplet contains a reference to God's word(s),
all that is, bar one

try reading Aleph aloud lifting your hand when God's Word is mentioned
see it represented by one of these ten words: laws, statutes, precepts, commands,
testimonies, judgements, oracle, the Word, the way of God or righteousness

now more about those couplets
the second line will either extend or contrast the thought presented in the first line,
this device lifts meaning and emphasis

as we read all 176 verses the modules and couplets make up a pattern
like a pattern repeat in a roll of wallpaper
think of steps in a formal dance, movements of repetition
it's a teaching ploy to help us remember

try reading Aleph as a response with someone else - feel the movement as you
read . . . . . enjoy the experience of reading it aloud
listen to the writer tossing thoughts back and forth in the couplets

all 22 modules are facets of spiritual life, and are laid out as a progression
or perhaps a building, brick by brick, each brick with eight fixing lugs
interlocking couplets, like Lego bricks,
         . . . . . . being part of a structured conversation with God

contents

meeting God

Aleph

Psalm 119 : 1 - 8

Oh that my ways
may be steadfast

Aleph

1
Blessed are those whose way is blameless,
who walk in the law of the Lord!

2
Blessed are those who keep his testimonies,
who seek him with their whole heart,

3
who also do no wrong,
but walk in his ways!

4
You have commanded your precepts
to be kept diligently.

5
Oh that my ways may be steadfast
in keeping your statutes!

6
Then I shall not be put to shame,
having my eyes fixed on all your commandments.

7
I will praise you with an upright heart,
when I learn your righteous rules.

8
I will keep your statutes;
do not utterly forsake me!

the appeal of happiness

prelude

while Moses was keeping sheep in the Sinai Peninsula he saw a bush on fire, this
was not unusual in those parts
but what caught his attention was the fact that the bush was not consumed
he went across for a closer look

God spoke to Moses from the burning bush
they went on to have a conversation about future days

while this sounds fantastic
many of us would like the opportunity Moses had
we too would like a one to one with God

Psalm 119 was written by another shepherd, David
this David's whole life seemed like a conversation with God
you can read about his good times and his bad times so neatly recorded for us in
the beautiful 23rd Psalm

God also inspired David to write this 119th Psalm for us in our day and here he
gives us an insight into his long relationship with God
he gives us an insight into a life that was a conversation with God

this may sound fantastic
until we begin our own conversation with God
a God who can give light and understanding to anyone who comes for a closer look

the contrast

the first thing we read about in the Psalm are happy and contented people
we imagine the writer seeing those people,
all so happy and not putting a foot wrong
then he blurts out 'Oh I wish I could be like that and I'm not
I'm so disappointed as I review my life'

see the contrast
vs1-4 a review of happy believers
vs5-8 the complaint as the writer reviews himself

this is typical poetic spotlight, bringing recognition by contrast
without the datum point of vs1-4 the writer could remain content
saying 'I'm as good and as happy as I need to be'
now he is confronted with exquisitely happy believers while he is unhappy and feels
regret and sorrow

our common practice is to look around on our level and choose a datum point
and to say 'I'm as good as', or 'I'm better than' others
first lesson in the 119 manual; look at a different role model
the currency here is God's Word and how we compare

the test for us is, are we content, are we happy?
Aleph is a door at street level for everyone
no one is excluded here
I'm for signing up for the next 21 sessions
at the same time asking, where could that take me?

a wobbly place

t seems our writer is feeling neither steadfast or firm v5
n stark contrast to those he sees who 'do nothing wrong' vs1-4
f our thinking lacks firm qualities
our subsequent behaviour will follow the same pattern
contributing to the choices we will make

to be steadfast is to be resolute
a clear directive set by God as demonstrated in v1
the wobbly place is not resolute . . . period   read James 1: 5-8[1]
the nature of our 'choice' behaviour is contaminated with uncertainty
flowing from a conflict in our allegiance

for example, Eve was in a wobbly place by the tree in Eden
she said 'God said,' His spoken words are true
sadly, this statement was in conflict with her desire, which overrode her fine words
and she eats the fruit
so, when visited later by God, her action brought on shame

notice v6 where shame follows failure to obey
oh that I was steadfast, presupposes doubt, and failure to believe due to the
alternating hierarchy of two masters
a fluctuating compliance . . . .a wobbly place to be

the options are
the vs1-4 person - recognises God's quality and value over self and has passed
control over to God as the wiser path
the vs5-8 person - recognises God's quality and value over self but has retained the
right to veto

> sometimes I obey sometimes I don't
> now, where am I, ... and what is my position?

resolve

for some ... the journey begins here
we see in v7 and v8 that the future tense *I will*, reveals a new beginning
between v5 and v6 something happens, resolve happens in that space
the possibility of moving from shame to steadfast becomes a reality
.....an expedition is envisaged!

is there a place near God's heart for me to be? ... can I change where I am?
more important, do I want to make the journey whatever it costs
because I really want to be blessed?
let's see Psalm 119 as 22 stages on that journey, a route laid out for us with
signposts and markers on the way.

the writer here is keen to encourage action, by setting out the contrast
to show a better place for us to be
to discover way marks and companions for the adventure
but he is not able to implant 'resolve'   that's for us to do ourselves

we have an imaginary turnstile here - will you step through?
beyond are dangers, enemies to fight, disappointments, labour and pain
we have an experienced guide, who will lead us to the throne room of God the Father
we have an imaginary turnstile here - will you step through?

we think for a moment .....we hesitate because we know it's true
God is as good as His word
we will be changed when we seek Him with all our heart
and that is the problem ... a fear of the unknown

remember, we are not alone
we are not utterly forsaken v8

to do

try this initial activity to test the water

. . . . I will praise consistently as I learn v7

our apathy may have wearied our Saviour somewhat
but He is still on board, we are not utterly forsaken
as creatures of dubious habits we are in need of help here
His hand is outstretched toward us to assist
and rest assured we are going to need it

beginning from a standing start we are probably a bit feeble
v7 seems to offer a suggestion for the beginner
praise while learning . . . that's praise with mind and heart engaged
being careful to get whole self into gear - consciously done
learning the theory and the experience together

perhaps a taster from the prophet Habakkuk will help
he lived in very bleak times - yet he would praise
read Habakkuk 3: 17-19 *Yet will I rejoice in the Lord* [2]
let's practice getting whole self in unison with praise
let's not overestimate our contribution
let's humble ourselves before God
in bleak times when our hands are empty
yet we will praise
begin to learn
be my strength for the journey
enable me to tread the heights!

step away from the comfort zone
let's do this with resolve
and next we'll make a plan together . . . . .

footnotes

1
James 1: 5-8
If any of you lacks wisdom, let him ask
God, who gives generously to all without
reproach, and it will be given him. But let
him ask in faith, with no doubting, for the
one who doubts is like a wave of the sea
that is driven and tossed by the wind. For
that person must not suppose that he
will receive anything from the Lord; he is
a double-minded man, unstable in all his
ways.

2
Habakkuk 3: 17-19
Though the fig tree should not blossom,
    nor fruit be on the vines,
the produce of the olive fail
    and the fields yield no food,
the flock be cut off from the fold
    and there be no herd in the stalls,
yet I will rejoice in the Lord;
    I will take joy in the God of my salvation.
God, the Lord, is my strength;
    he makes my feet like the deer's;
    he makes me tread on my high places.

Beth

Psalm 119 : 9 -16

How can a young man
keep his way pure?

Beth

9
How can a young man keep his way pure?
By guarding it according to your word.

10
With my whole heart I seek you;
let me not wander from your commandments!

11
I have stored up your word in my heart,
that I might not sin against you.

12
Blessed are you, O Lord;
teach me your statutes!

13
With my lips I declare
all the rules of your mouth.

14
In the way of your testimonies I delight
as much as in all riches.

15
I will meditate on your precepts
and fix my eyes on your ways.

16
I will delight in your statutes;
I will not forget your word.

changing mindset

asking the question

pre flight energy

keeping focus

a powerful propellant

the list

asking the question

in Aleph there was a distinct contrast between two sorts of people
firstly, those who are happy make a connection with God's words
and live in accord with it
then there were others, like the writer, who were living moment by moment
without purpose

this prompted the question in v9 *How can a young man keep his way pure*?
from the context we assume the question is genuine
expecting a positive solution
it suggests resolve .. an intention to make a change

who is being asked the question?
God is being asked, this is a conversation with God we heard about
and the answer is
by living according to your words

vs10-16 sets out a plan of action to progress in the best spiritual sense

the proposal is that by living in step with the Bible - trying to keep in step with the
words of God like two people interlocked together in a three legged race, you
become one with the other and surely success will follow

but not all is straight forward

pre flight energy

escaping gravitational pull is, in a variety of ways, expensive
in a similar way it is hard work leaving established habits and mindsets

vs10-11 reveal early conflicts between the new resolve and the old behaviour
v11 is a good plan seeing a progression to the next 3 couplets
vs12-15 seem to embody more harmony with both lines of the couplet in
agreement   there is real progression

in Aleph we resolved to make a change
frankly ashamed of our previous performance
our mindset (our established set of attitudes) contained doubts
and weak objectives that manifested a lack of steadfastness

we are now looking for a change of mindset, and God can help us with that
resolve is needed, and that means behaving in a way that is at odds with our old
mindset to prove our resolve to be genuine

Beth points the way to go ... here is the initial plan

seeking God with every ounce of desire available
                                while old mindset is still tugging elsewhere
driving His words deep into our being as a datum
                        to deter wrong actions
positive praise as a soundtrack while pleading for spiritual input

how serious are we? God needs to see we are serious
look at Matthew 9: 27-29[1], see how eager those blind men were
even when Jesus goes indoors they follow Him there
they were persistent - do we believe enough to persist

is our faith big enough to take us through the hard bit
pre flight is full power taxiing with no flight - but committed to flight

keeping focus

with those blind men, Jesus touched their eyes and sight was restored.
here in Beth vs13-15 is a rising thermal - towards a synergy with God
t looks and sounds so attractive

t is true, but at a price
t means sacrificing more of self to gain wings and eyes that see

not a two tiered Christian experience of super holiness
ust solid growth as a believer
n v9 it's a matter of actively keeping his way pure
the 'way' or the 'path' leads on higher while we tend to live on a convenient plateau,
gnoring the onward path ... Beth will have none of that

t may begin with expended energy but it moves on to deeper things

ook at the attentiveness in v13 *my lips .. Your mouth*, we are close
oy is now transferred, finding its rest on a higher plane v14
my mind is content and caressed by God's words v15
now it appears there is no longer a fight to focus on holy things
n John Bunyan's book, Grace Abounding, he talks about sitting in the sun with other
believers[2]
can we believe there is a sunnier place to be, in that place close to the Saviour

n Aleph we felt dissatisfaction with our life, and we chose 'resolve'
now synergy with the mind and words of God seems like joy
t seems like a prize worth working for
although that's true, remember our blind people in Matthew who wanted their eyes
opened - is our view of glory still impaired?

ooking ahead to Gimel, v18 we read 'open my eyes that I might see' indicating that
perhaps there is more in store

a powerful propellant

we find that in v16, I do this .... so I won't do that
maybe there is more going on here than we first thought?
is there an active propellant taking me forward that I was not aware of?

our psalm begins with the action in this way
the axiom, a self evident truth, could look like this:-
1. desire and resolve   2. resolve in action   3. resolve rewarded
a cycle of truth
a cycle of combustion fired by the Spirit of God
this is repeated, again and again, this is the principle of spiritual life

fortunately, as we shall see we are not alone in this cycle
for in reality   Christ shows me my need for resolve
                      I apply to Christ with integrity
                      Christ fulfils my request
like an Archimedean screw   lifting me higher and nearer

in Aleph vs5-6 failure and disappointment in past life was recognised
now that isn't natural - in fact it's the working of the Spirit of God Himself
be encouraged, seriously encouraged
God Almighty is showing you He cares about you
                                    because He is working in you

nurture that life like a gardener nurtures a precious seedling
be attentive to the Holy Spirit within - who leads you on
ask the giver of life and sight to nurture you and then follow His words

I will delight in your statutes
I will not forget your word v16

this is first hand experience and words of a first hand user
albeit a few thousand years ago, but no matter, the things of God are timeless

the list

here is Beth : written as a list of things to do

1. solve the problem
how can the young, or any sort of person stay on the path of purity?
Live according to Your Word - as we read our Bible
Believe that things will change

2. a plan of action
seek the Lord with integrity, be industrious
stockpile God's Word, design methods to accumulate it
praise, if we feel like it or not

3. monitor change
observe a harmonisation developing
see a change of allegiance in our joy placement
note how the mind dwells naturally on the Word

4 keep on the path
understand there is no limit to growth
don't stop on a plateau when the path continues
no neglect - keep driving on

footnotes

1
Matthew 9 : 27-29
And as Jesus passed on from there, two blind men followed him, crying aloud, "Have mercy on us, Son of David." When he entered the house, the blind men came to him, and Jesus said to them, "Do you believe that I am able to do this?" They said to him, "Yes, Lord." Then he touched their eyes, saying, "According to your faith be it done to you."

2
John Bunyan, Grace Abounding
41. About this time, the state and happiness of these poor people at Bedford was thus in a Dream or Vision represented to me: I saw as if they were set on the Sunny side of some high Mountain, there refreshing themselves with the pleasant beams of the Sun, while I was shivering and shrinking in the cold, afflicted with frost, snow, and dark clouds; methought also betwixt me and them I saw a wall that did compass about this Mountain; now this wall, my Soul did greatly desire to pass, concluding that if I could, I would go even into the very midst of them, and there also comfort my self with the heat of their Sun.

Gimel

Psalm 119 : 17-24

I am a sojourner
on the earth

Gimel

17
Deal bountifully with your servant,
that I may live and keep your word.

18
Open my eyes, that I may behold
wondrous things out of your law.

19
I am a sojourner on the earth;
hide not your commandments from me!

20
My soul is consumed with longing
for your rules at all times.

21
You rebuke the insolent, accursed ones,
who wander from your commandments.

22
Take away from me scorn and contempt,
for I have kept your testimonies.

23
Even though princes sit plotting against me,
your servant will meditate on your statutes.

24
Your testimonies are my delight;
they are my counsellors.

in a different world

two views

Gimel generalises two views of how people relate to God
>   those who take him seriously vs17-20
>   and those who do not v21

notice in v19 the writer sees himself now as a stranger on the earth
no longer at one with the majority, but someone just passing through

how has this change come about?
in Aleph, a divided trust between earthly and spiritual values led him to be unstable
and unhappy
in Beth, he began to keep himself pure by seriously seeking fellowship with his maker
in Gimel, he discovers that the more he is 'connected' to the eternal God the more
'temporary' is his relationship with the earth
it's a train of events

his unhappiness in Aleph, drove him to earnest devotion in Beth, resulting in a
mindset shift in Gimel

the earthbound are masters of their own destiny v21
as opposed to our man who in v17 humbly asks God to be generous just so he
might live - he now sees himself as dependent on God

this is an immense shift in mindset
>   our man here longs for God, wants to live for Him and His name
>   in direct contrast to those who do not take God seriously
thus in v19 he says, 'I'm a sojourner': a real sense of being different
it seems our man has crossed the Rubicon, no longer ashamed with doubts
>   no longer earth bound
but connected to his Redeemer with a genuine longing to be with Him
>   and thus clearly heaven bound
with a temporary lodging here en route to an eternity with God's perfect love

we are seeing God from two viewpoints that are poles apart

dependence

we see at once our man displaying total dependence on God for life, obedience and sight in vs17-18

the beatitudes in Matthew 5¹ speak about poverty of spirit and an awareness of spiritual helplessness that takes us to our knees in prayer as we see in our man here

> but he is not in despair or giving up
> nor does he redefine the situation to match his ability

we see what things God requires of us in terms of faith, belief and actions and maybe recognise that this does not match our natural abilities

options are   recalibrate the requirements
         admit poverty and ask God to supply our lack

when God seems to ask the impossible, remember Augustine of Hippo
he said 'God, give what you command, and command what you will'

v17 repeats the sentiment *'that I may live and keep your word'*
or, God, please do 'x' that I will be able to do 'y'
natural life and spiritual life with a common objective

'deal bountifully', generously .. assumes an awareness of bankruptcy
I'm dead so deal me life
v18 open my eyes, . . . I can't see

> I'm blind - open my eyes
> I'm blind - make me see

our man wants   a new orientation towards God
         and an ability to see and grasp spiritual concepts

the hope is   to source the ability to obey
         to experience the truth and wealth of the written Word

a move from managing his own destiny to childlike dependence

deep longing

we easily see that v20 is about love
here is a reference to 'Beth's' new place of steadfastness
a result of that cycle of change, seeing beauty and possibility in God
awareness of a shifting of hope, a future with new objectives
alongside a growing disillusionment with earthly values, of being out of sync with
everyone because of my attraction to God
and my unaccountable but persistent longing for something beyond

when mindful of our parents Adam and Eve and their expulsion from God's side
and the garden of Eden because of their arrogance
it's not surprising that we feel a deep longing to return to our Maker

the last module saw an upsurge in effort and desire to be nearer to God *with my
whole heart I will seek you'* v10
and an increasing sense of synergy in the whole person

having cast off from one shore
he longs for a new and better shore
all is committed to an arrival ..... he is a spiritual migrant

again, my soul is consumed with longing, v20
overwhelmed with a desire for the speaker of those words

think
as believers, what is my affinity with others, are we strangers on the earth
do we struggle with our feelings ..... like some spiritual puberty as we are changed
do we look round for encouragement, to confirm that it's alright

with this sense of being different
he looked to the Word and found that confirmation

local environment

from that spiritual embrace we turn and see the alternative
see what is natural for others, the contrast is highlighted in vs21-23

the norm in society is to see belief in God as superfluous - even unhealthy
religion is fine, provided it is hollowed out to be a sentimental affection
or a mystical concoction of our own making

it's fine that we are masters of our own planet and destiny
assured that we are not dependent beings .... and quite sure that
medieval deities are not required to prop up our contemporary lives

our man on the other hand
only lived because of God's generosity v17
convinced that to be otherwise would be a supreme arrogance
namely a rejection of God's   as in v21b

a worrying sense of identity with the old mindset reappears
take away from me scorn and contempt v22
he recoils at the sight of his failings
I've been there, I know that place ...... remove those traits from me Lord
give me the good things, take away my bad things, for I am helpless

here's the difference
while they sit and concoct slanders, gossip and negative opinions
your servant .... will feed on your decrees, the attributes of your person

the local surroundings reveal the difference

early dissatisfaction with doubt and weakness led him to a place where
he latches on to God with integrity and now he is experiencing a deep longing for
the Redeemer, while at odds with his surroundings

with enlightened sight the old surroundings even now urge him to paths of humility
and desire

wondrous things

your testimonies are my delight; they are my counsellors v24
this stranger in the world is delighting in God's words

Matthew 6: 24 no one can serve two masters. either you will hate the one and love the other, or you will be devoted to the one and despise the other

this devotion accepts God's directives … they are my counsellors
these words reveal synergy and devotion

the cause of that lack of steadfastness in Aleph has now been sorted
he is under new management
happy, content with the harmony of his soul with God as master
and God's words as counsellor

so we must ask, where are we in life?
remember
Aleph: a partial trust in earthly values led him to be unstable and unhappy
Beth: asks can I keep pure by seriously seeking fellowship with my Maker
Gimel: the more 'connected' I am with eternal God the more 'temporary' is my relationship with the earth

it is incredible to the natural man that total compliance with God's Word results in delight, that very experience is the claim of the man who wrote these lines

so the majority may not be right
when our eyes are open and we can see wondrous things, the old blind guides will never convince us it's better otherwise!

footnotes

I

Matthew 5: 2-8
And he opened his mouth and taught
them, saying:

"Blessed are the poor in spirit, for theirs is
the kingdom of heaven.

"Blessed are those who mourn, for they
shall be comforted.

"Blessed are the meek, for they shall
inherit the earth.

"Blessed are those who hunger and
thirst for righteousness, for they shall be
satisfied.

"Blessed are the merciful, for they shall
receive mercy.

"Blessed are the pure in heart, for they
shall see God.

Daleth

Psalm 119 : 25-32

Give me life
according to
your word!

Daleth

25
My soul clings to the dust;
give me life according to your word!

26
When I told of my ways, you answered me;
teach me your statutes!

27
Make me understand the way of your precepts,
and I will meditate on your wondrous works.

28
My soul melts away for sorrow;
strengthen me according to your word!

29
Put false ways far from me
and graciously teach me your law!

30
I have chosen the way of faithfulness;
I set your rules before me.

31
I cling to your testimonies, O Lord;
let me not be put to shame!

32
I will run in the way of your commandments
when you enlarge my heart!

rescue me

biting the dust

give me life

melted by sorrow

the word is dabaq

living to run

biting the dust

up till now we were doing so well
we had a plan and everything was fine
now look
he says I'm overwhelmed by exhaustion, I'm dead
awash with shame and deceit, I'm finished - Lord, please resurrect me v25

we have a confession as well as exhaustion
he is in a bleak place along with the realisation that following God is not just about
resolve, it's about repentance

it's not just a bad day, a blip in the witness and back on to it tomorrow
no, he has 'bitten the dust' a phrase defined as to die or to end in failure
look at Psalm 72: 9 for more of that dust
may the desert tribes bow before him and his enemies lick the dust.

v25 sounds like being 'buried' and 'dust to dust' is a phrase we hear at funerals
straight away he calls out to his God *'give me life'*
we open Daleth with our hero, dead or at least totally incapacitated
saying please restore my life (my life is in God's hand to restore)

obvious questions
is this just a hiccup on the road to glory?
or is it an episode that qualifies us to find that glory?

how is this wreck of humanity to be understood with all his good intentions?
what life are we enjoying, does it compare with 'life according to God's Word'?

give me life

in this module Daleth, we have a 5-3 split
vs25-29 a realisation of death, blindness and a dysfunctional nature
vs30-32 a realisation of the need for a heart change with an injection of new life

the key point here is that this request is made while at his lowest point in v25
by myself I cannot do this, I am paralysed, dead and helpless
this real awareness of inability triggers a genuine call for life

the initial strut into christian life based on a personal plan must fail
this is such a disappointment!
failure is depressing see v28 weary with trying and not achieving
Christ's requests are unattainable to the spiritually blind due to our father Adam
whose fall brought us all into this state

give me life implies an external injection that will save him from ruin
by nature, our spiritual abilities are paralysed
in Mark 2¹ Jesus' touch is joined to forgiveness as he heals the paralysed man

our realisation of need . . . is an essential stage in salvation
our spirit must be reborn in us as a contemporary miracle
we kneel before our Saviour and confess our sin and failure, then ask for life

in v26 *I told* . . . a true confession of failure will bring an answer from our Lord
try to visualise the concept. - you inviting God to reconfigure your core mechanism
conversion is just that, God making real changes to your abilities and understanding

it's far more than you turning over a new leaf

v27 . . .*make me understand*
please override my sin driven paralysis - open my blind eyes
                    Lord, I must be born again

melted by sorrow

there is a pivotal concept revealed in v28
it is the cycle of being both broken and sustained
I am feeble and washed out with sorrow and sin   .. and always imbibing life giving
righteousness from Christ

without the brokenness .... natural pride and arrogance take the lead
you can see God hates pride when you think of Christ as a manifestation of God
how He was humbled beyond all measure in His birth and death

now here, enlightened, I grasp my natural status and am weary with sorrow
strengthen me says v28, according to Your Word, Your promise
Christ is our righteousness, living in us, all our love and ability flows from this union

v28 again not according to my request but according to Your Word
our paltry expectation is best ignored, instead all is supplied by the Creator's word
as He enters our being, He answers according to His fullness - overwhelming

unfaithfulness is a recurring problem that finds a constant solution
the believer, here in this life, can know a constant filling and refreshing

the church is no reservoir, it is a channel - thus always being filled
generating praise, devotion, love and prayer

the word is dabaq

read vs29-31
here is faith and trust in action alongside an awareness of our dysfunctional nature

saying
I know that in my thinking I am always liable to be deceitful, please be gracious and keep me from my own tendency - even my own mind is not to be trusted, it may give me false positives
please manage the overrides where needed to keep me true - your WORD will guide me

every day I am prone to things that will bring shame on Your Name
I find my will powerful and persuasive
so may Your indwelling presence hold sway and enable me to 'hold fast'
    ..... do not let me fail

there is emphasis in the Hebrew word dabaq. to *'cling to'*
I *'cling to'* v31 (dabaq) *your testimonies*
back in v25 we had *'I cling'* to the dust; 'dabaq' is the Hebrew word again
a tug of war between clinging to the dust and clinging to God
and here we need the power of God indwelling us to enable us to overcome

do not let me down - extend grace to enable me
Paul tells us about the extent of the battle, read about it in Ephesians 6:10-20[2]

pride will try to convince us that we can manage by ourselves

but no, we are deeply in need of Christ's saving power
clinging is the word ... it's dabaq

living to run

when God works in our hearts He gives us life and vigour
Ezekiel 36: 26 tells us   *And I will give you a new heart, and a new spirit I will put within you. And I will remove the heart of stone from your flesh and give you a heart of flesh*
Matthew 16: 25 Jesus said *For whoever would save his life will lose it, but whoever loses his life for my sake will find it*
this is a new testament rendering of our old testament Daleth notion
it's Daleth thinking

at the beginning of this Daleth module
he was
clinging to a dead thing, *give me life* he said according to Your word
then he was resurrected and renewed . . .this is the way to go
with self seen in its true colours, a new heart supplied, life is without boundaries.
this is life according to Your boundless word
 according to' means to be packaged in line with God's super generous spirit

so the Daleth module is about seeing the goodness of God
at the same time recognising our own persistent ingrained disinterest in
worship and prayer
> telling God about the truth of our apathy v26
> the reality of the collateral damage resulting from Adam's fall so evident in our spiritual lack of life and sight

let's not trust ourselves
> ask Him for life 'according' to His boundless Word
> give our lives over to Christ - His ways, His understanding can be ours

christian living will be no drudge, trying to keep it up
we've given up trying on our own, we know that's hopeless
we've asked for life, new life
now we will run in His ways .. because He lives in us

footnotes

1
Mark 2: 8b-11
"Why do you question these things in your hearts? 9 Which is easier, to say to the paralytic, 'Your sins are forgiven', or to say, 'Rise, take up your bed and walk'? 10 But that you may know that the Son of Man has authority on earth to forgive sins"—he said to the paralytic— "I say to you, rise, pick up your bed, and go home."

2
Ephesians 6 : 10-20
Finally, be strong in the Lord and in the strength of his might. Put on the whole armour of God, that you may be able to stand against the schemes of the devil. For we do not wrestle against flesh and blood, but against the rulers, against the authorities, against the cosmic powers over this present darkness, against the spiritual forces of evil in the heavenly places. Therefore take up the whole armour of God, that you may be able to withstand in the evil day, and having done all, to stand firm. Stand therefore, having fastened on the belt of truth, and having put on the breastplate of righteousness, and, as shoes for your feet, having put on the readiness given by the gospel of peace. In all circumstances take up the shield of faith, with which you can extinguish all the flaming darts of the evil one; and take the helmet of salvation, and the sword of the Spirit, which is the word of God, praying at all times in the Spirit, with all prayer and supplication. To that end keep alert with all perseverance, making supplication for all the saints, and also for me, that words may be given to me in opening my mouth boldly to proclaim the mystery of the gospel, for which I am an ambassador in chains, that I may declare it boldly, as I ought to speak.

He

Psalm 119 : 33 - 40

Turn my eyes from
looking at worthless things

He

33
Teach me, O Lord, the way of your statutes;
and I will keep it to the end.

34
Give me understanding, that I may keep your law
and observe it with my whole heart.

35
Lead me in the path of your commandments,
for I delight in it.

36
Incline my heart to your testimonies,
and not to selfish gain!

37
Turn my eyes from looking at worthless things;
and give me life in your ways.

38
Confirm to your servant your promise,
that you may be feared.

39
Turn away the reproach that I dread,
for your rules are good.

40
Behold, I long for your precepts;
in your righteousness give me life!

the new partnership

new horizons

discipline to delight

head turner

sea change

a vision of delights

new horizons

earlier endeavours at steadfastness have failed
then a sense of brokenness brought a realisation of need and help is sought
'give me life' he prayed and v32 reflects a genuine change of heart

as new born believers we co-habit with God himself - needless to say, some
readjustments are required and the 'He' module is about compliance and focus
within this new found life

coming to grips with this new partnership with God involves change
how will the needy supplicant and the Saviour understand each other?
mental and spiritual reconfigurations are in progress
it is extraordinary to be in a working partnership with our Saviour - so unlike our
previous lone experience

how do we visualise v33
teach me O Lord the way of your statutes, or give me understanding
just how will that actually happen   .....
what is the nature of that interaction with God

is it just a checklist, will it be multiple choice answers or will I have to go up the
front for role play

if I ask God to *'teach me'* what will happen ...will anything actually happen?

discipline to delight

it is no small matter to abandon old life strategies and build a new life with God
the personal revisions in this section establish more than a hint of what is involved
in the future

nevertheless we get a real sense of energy and integrity in his prayer
this is not just being mouthed as a pious idea
it's a proposed action to be implemented for it to actually happen

keeping up with his sense of urgency is crucial
because any mutual 'teaching exercise' is a reciprocal arrangement
you teach - I'll learn is the agreement
the module reveals genuine commitment embedded in the request
one that is active and experimental
his enthusiasm for movement and discovery is infectious

he and God together ..... are working on an appraisal of the past and a plan for
the future
God in perfect love and holiness entwined with our man .....both relishing the
objective while recognising new heavenly resources funding the needed energy and
resolve to carry out the work

the movement from self driven behaviour to Christlike behaviour is obvious
the excitement is about reform and Godliness
which in turn wonderfully pans out into 'freedom' and delight' as per v35

shall we ask God to teach us?
can you imagine such a partnership with God to renew your spiritual life?
can this module mean anything else ...

head turner

look at the remodelling happening in vs36-37
there are priority changes of the will
turning away from things . . . is proof of an altered mindset
this is certainly not a superficial whitewash job

the selfish gain department in v36 so besotted with worthless things in v37,
will need a powerful attraction to divert its attention from old loves
an attraction not unlike the moon which is able to turn tides this way and that

our new friend and confidant the Lord Himself is well experienced in jobs like
turning tidal flows, He does it all the time
our prayerful converse will be 'please turn my heart and eyes - I don't have the
desire or ability to overcome my own will, help me to prioritise, to seek first the
kingdom of heaven'

Abraham of old had material goods aplenty, but they did not rule him, he was
looking in a different direction, beyond it all
his head was turned to another city, the dwelling place of his God[1]

now that the personal love and thinking mechanisms are recommissioned
by our Lord, with objectives reconfigured, everything changes
we are not just painting the train a new colour - we have put it on completely
different tracks

here we are being encouraged to face the same way as God
the exciting part is that we get to work with One who can turn tides and such
opportunities are not part of the everyday

sea change

consider the scale and magnitude of what we are involved in, you and I are collaborating with God, the creator of the universe
just you and He - a turner of tides, effecting a sea change in your life v38
God himself involved in realigning the axis of your thinking to now major on spiritua targets

incoming

our man is asking for sustained confirmation as an encouragement v38
he is in new territory
he has risked everything - thus he says
I want to experience the change as I kneel as a servant
I am kneeling, please deliver
the delivery of God's power is expected
and naturally I will revere and respect Your majesty for ever

outgoing

rid me of uncertainty that looms ahead, remember I was unstable v39
fill me with the confidence that Your power in me will enable me to hold course so that I will not fail You with relapsed thinking

because Your ways, Your laws are the best

our man and God are building together, a harmony of purpose
job sharing according to ability
God doing all the heavy lifting
and our man loving to do everything he can
and doing it together

a vision of delights

we have a beautiful long view of Christ's work on Calvary
at the time of writing this Psalm 119 the solution for sin is in the future . . .like
Abraham looking for the future city not made with hands
the phrase 'long for' is the same as 'love for' what God has promised
wonderfully we today have full sight of it, we have the gospels
we have the Holy Spirit, we have so much

little knowing the full new testament glory from his old testament time frame he
opens the words *in your righteousness give me life* v40
give me impetus, give me holy energy, open my eyes, direct my paths etc

here's our man - 10th century BC engaged in this little and large partnership
never thinking his infinite, extra terrestrial partner will come to terra firma
to load Himself with our vile contagious sin and die for us
so that . . we are completely freed of sin's power

the promise is confirmed, it is done v38
our disgrace is taken away, it is done v39
Christ is our righteousness, we must be in Him or die [2]
we must revere

this is His Word to us
our man longed for His precepts v40
we have it in our hand!   what do you think about that?
we have the promise of meeting Christ
let's learn from our man
let's have a longing for our Lord

footnotes

1
Hebrews 11:8-10
By faith Abraham obeyed when he was
called to go out to a place that he was to
receive as an inheritance. And he went out,
not knowing where he was going. By faith
he went to live in the land of promise, as in
a foreign land, living in tents with Isaac and
Jacob, heirs with him of the same promise.
For he was looking forward to the city
that has foundations, whose designer and
builder is God.

2
Hebrews 10:19-23
Therefore, brothers, since we have
confidence to enter the holy places by
the blood of Jesus, by the new and living
way that he opened for us through the
curtain, that is, through his flesh, and since
we have a great priest over the house of
God, let us draw near with a true heart
in full assurance of faith, with our hearts
sprinkled clean from an evil conscience
and our bodies washed with pure water.
Let us hold fast the confession of our hope
without wavering, for he who promised is
faithful.

Waw

Psalm 119 : 41 - 48

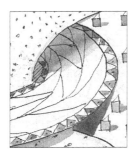

Let your
steadfast love
come to me, O Lord

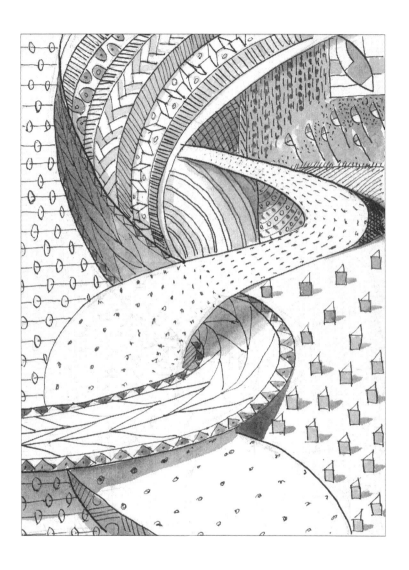

Waw

41

Let your steadfast love come to me, O Lord,
your salvation according to your promise;

42

then shall I have an answer for him who taunts me,
for I trust in your word.

43

And take not the word of truth utterly out of my mouth,
for my hope is in your rules.

44

I will keep your law continually,
forever and ever,

45

and I shall walk in a wide place,
for I have sought your precepts.

46

I will also speak of your testimonies before kings
and shall not be put to shame,

47

for I find my delight in your commandments,
which I love.

48

I will lift up my hands toward your commandments, which I love,
and I will meditate on your statutes.

asking for love

the love of God

be my voice

unhindered freedom

I'm in love with God

a consuming passion

the love of God

in the previous module we asked to be taught by the Lord himself
to have understanding and for power to overcome personal failures
we wanted to be in a place where we actually longed for the Lord

in this module we are on a high - fuelled by a surge of love for God Himself
blithely unaware of bleaker times ahead, the writer is overflowing with love and
enthusiasm
we cannot help but ask - can we love like that?
at best our love is patchy, perhaps a little dilute
is this psalm for real, or is it a melodramatic, overblown idealism that is not for the
likes of ordinary people?

but remember, Psalm 119 is a carefully crafted teaching aid, arranged in a way to
help us grasp elements of faith in a living God
the building blocks of reality . . . albeit a spiritual reality

in v41
the initial request is that God's love and salvation would flow into him to fill him
a concept we find reflected in new testament terminology, see Romans 5[1]
so it would appear that on a heartfelt request - one could experience heavenly
sluice gates opening, and love pouring into our hearts
love that is amazing in its volume and effect
a mighty inrush of God's love vs41- 48

in this module, this effect is examined in three parts
> vs42-43 be my voice
> vs44-45 unhindered freedom
> vs46-47 in love with God

showing us the transforming effect of incoming salvation and love
and that this is reality
the prayer of v41 is phenomenal

be my voice

in vs42-43 we notice that everything is subject to God
we read about God's words, their words and taunts and my words
'for' occurs here twice, meaning 'consequently', a complete trust in God's words
thus the confidence in vs42-43, is not from ourself, it is derived from trusting
the phrase *an answer* in v42 has its origin in the idea of vibrancy and confidence

v43 assumes that the words in his mouth are inspired by God
invert the negative phrase to a positive and it would say 'maintain Your word of
truth flowing from my mouth'

what does that actually mean in layman's terms?
it means that our God is now not a passive resident in our being
He is being invited to influence our departments of thinking and speaking
His wisdom is perfect and our reasoning will follow from that

again v43 *for my hope is in your rules*
　　　　my hope is my eternal certainty
　　　　your rules are God's words as they express His thinking

thus my future certainty is placed in the peerless thinking of God
　　　　my thinking is inferior to God's perfect thinking
　　　　so I'll place my future in His thinking

to understand this we have to understand God as resident within us
not a remote figure, like a distant being in historic literature

v43, *take not the word of truth ... out of my mouth* means I depend on God for
inspiration and utterance so him who taunts me v42, especially Satan our enemy,
can be answered

unhindered freedom

I will always obey v44 and I will walk about in a wide place that is freedom v45

we want to see those words and thoughts applied to our current situation
we are looking around at each other as the local material

God does not taunt us with the impossible - this is Him leading us by the hand
beyond our current experience
when in v41 unfailing love and salvation came to him
he is speaking about the average us,
> about the Holy Spirit who has been given to us Romans 5:5[1]
> average us recognising Bethlehem love, Calvary love and Resurrection
> love poured into us
> now try to calibrate an average response to that profound thought!!

the 'I will obey' of v44 is not a self orientated agenda for our religious behaviour
it is more like someone united to their living Lord,
someone wallowing in an influx of God's bountiful love

ink these thoughts with that moment when Peter was walking on water[2]
Jesus said 'with eyes only on me - walk on water - look away and you'll sink'

walking about unhindered by sin to tempt us v45 is understood in this cycle
> the greater our synergy with Christ
> the greater is our desire to obey
> then the greater our freedom (from sin's influence)

the juxtaposition of obedience and freedom is significant
and notice obedience precedes freedom, obedience is a sort of fuel for unison and
by extension - freedom
Romans 6[3] speaks of being slaves to righteousness . . . or devoted to obedience

I'm in love with God

our current set of eight verses all roll together in the harmony of being devoted to the words of God
I will speak of your testimonies before kings v46
because I totally love these words along with the speaker of them
I'll boast about Him to anyone … it's a rising thermal
and v47 sees delight flow from love
my delight he says I am ecstatic, full on happy with God

we understand God is love .. and all love flows from God, therefore any love for God, also flows from God
even so we are not spectators here nor is it a form of spiritual archaeology, turning over the stones of the departed
the sheer delight the writer knew, 1000yrs later Paul knew and 2000yrs later we can know

the love of v47 is a first person love, *I love* because I am united with One whose love is poured into me
if we are lacking in love it's there for the asking
may your steadfast love come to me   let's say it ourselves

if God breathed life and breath into Adam at creation . . . . . and to us at birth when He imparted to us an eternal soul
can He, will He not, breath His love into us as well

what was that greatest commandment Jesus quoted to the rich young man
                    Love the Lord your God with all your heart, and soul[4]
how are we doing with that one?
                    may Your unfailing love (salvation) *come to me*
                    give me love to love You
then we will have everything to delight in, and everything to boast about,

a consuming passion

being animated by love is an eagerness for God himself
here in v48 is the reaching out and lifting up of hands
as one would reach for delicious nutritional food
to reach out for - love it and consume it - ingest it - repeat it
an insatiable appetite for what we love to meditate on

when love generates that appetite
we become willing enthusiasts for our Lord and His words
free, unhindered to follow where ever He leads us

revisit vs1-4 the blessed-blissfully happy
not a life of labour, toil and confinement
it's for you and me, and any who ask
may your steadfast love come to me

Lord, actually pour your love into my heart
so I can love with all my heart

and be ready for trouble ahead . . . . .

footnotes

1
Romans 5: 5
. . . . and hope does not put us to shame, because God's love has been poured into our hearts through the Holy Spirit who has been given to us.

2
Matthew 14: 29-31
He said, "Come." So Peter got out of the boat and walked on the water and came to Jesus. But when he saw the wind, he was afraid, and beginning to sink he cried out, "Lord, save me." Jesus immediately reached out his hand and took hold of him, saying to him, "O you of little faith, why did you doubt?"

3
Romans 6:17-18
. . . . but thanks be to God, that you who were once slaves of sin have become obedient from the heart to the standard of teaching to which you were committed, 18 and, having been set free from sin, have become slaves of righteousness.

4
Matthew 22: 36-37
"Teacher, which is the great commandment in the Law?" And he said to him, "You shall love the Lord your God with all your heart and with all your soul and with all your mind."

getting to know God

Zayin

Psalm 119 : 49 - 56

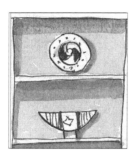

This is
my comfort in
my affliction

Zayin

49
Remember your word to your servant,
in which you have made me hope.

50
This is my comfort in my affliction,
that your promise gives me life.

51
The insolent utterly deride me,
but I do not turn away from your law.

52
When I think of your rules from of old,
I take comfort, O Lord.

53
Hot indignation seizes me because of the wicked,
who forsake your law.

54
Your statutes have been my songs
in the house of my sojourning.

55
I remember your name in the night, O Lord,
and keep your law.

56
This blessing has fallen to me,
that I have kept your precepts.

field test

a formula for life

road testing

hot indignation

in the dark

the path to joy

a formula for life

earlier, our writer experienced joy and love as he became immersed in God and His words
now, our excited believer is being gently lowered into an everyday world with all its rebellious aspects
a place where his God is rejected, reviled and he himself is mocked endlessly

in order to cope, he marks out three elements to keep in mind vs49-50
a steady tripod for unsteady ground

this is the formula for life and life abundant - essential information for that zip wire to glory

1. union with God God, your words are everything to me v49
the couplet is a plea and reminder together,
asking God to remember, while he is reminding himself
that all energy and worth flow from God,
he is happy to serve
his Lord will furnish things the willing servant needs

2. understanding this life we will even find comfort in suffering v50
our writer widens the scope from an internal conflict to an external conflict
experienced day by day
meeting the inevitable clash of values,
the clean amongst the unclean and the sheep among the wolves
placed in this physical discomfort we can rejoice in God's comfort applied to our heart

3. future proofed confidence we can know an eternal reality v50
my comfort in life is this, God's Covenant promise will deliver eternal certainty
this life is temporary, but eternal certainty comes wrapped in God's concrete promise of salvation
Christ is comfort now, and He is my passport to eternal bliss

this is the 119 formula for life and life abundant - the zip wire to glory

road testing

I think I have some anti mocking software in me that enables me to avoid being mocked and derided, I'm clever at ducking and diving . . . . . but

that is not what am I picking up from this text, it's about being rock solid in a situation where mocking is continuous and unrelenting
he keeps right on in line with God's instructions, staying faithful
a steady persistence - taking all the flack

the three legged formula that was set up in vs49-50 is seen here in action
this is road testing the theory
with mockers our natural reaction is to 'turn away' to avoid contact
not so here! v51b
unbelievably he turns 'mockers' into 'spiritual comfort' by holding course
quite simply he finds the spiritual reward for holding course is way better than ducking the incident
how so?

at the sight of a problem
with that promised help now flowing to him
along with that wonderful unfailing love . . remember v41
he rapidly does an appraisal of the everlasting words and promises uttered by his Lord
therefore, with promised help flowing to him meshing with a mental review of an eternal situation . . . he holds course

two things are experienced
while finite earthbound persons continue to deride our reputation and fidelity
we engage in a mental refresh of our Father's provisions and promises
we see right thinking along with right actions meshing together - a sense of comfort, rightness and peace ensue

to grimly do duty with clenched teeth does not work the same way
we need genuine fellowship and unison with our God to experience the 119 notion
we must get the indoor work on our relationship done before we step outside

hot indignation

on the one hand there is a reverence for and a loving of the words from our Lord,
be they commands, laws or promises
on the other hand there is a neglecting and an abandonment of the words
a trashing and a mocking of them
this mocking constitutes rebellion
we saw those who abandon the words mock those who keep those words

but what then is this *hot indignation* on the part of the believer? v53

God's words are part and parcel of Him who is the speaker
our relationship is personal, we love both the words spoken and the Speaker,
the two are one.
being surrounded by people who mock the one we love brings a reaction
when the infinite patience, love and forgiveness of our loved one is spurned and
trashed makes us indignant
we ourselves feel indignation at the insults heaped on our precious Lord

here we are again, repeating that foundational trio from vs49-50

this synchromeshing of our Lord with us sees His laws becoming a song in our
mouths
His requests are not tiresome - they are externalised in the form of song
happy stuff indeed

life (eternal) is the promise v50b life in a way that is valid beyond time!
a spiritual infusion to supersede our current understanding of life
it's clear we are heaven bound - just lodging here, only passing through this world

we find it repeats the tune we found at the beginning in vs49-50

1. when in unison with our beloved
2. we understand this life with its insults and character assassination
3. convinced our life is future proofed we find comfort regardless

in the dark

even when the mockers and the wicked have been managed
we turn to address another fear, the fear of the dark and the future

in the night we cannot see, and fears can overwhelm us
we find the streets at night to be different, let alone the woods
the future too is invisible to us - what lies ahead - we cannot know
our vulnerability to harm is real if that harm is not in view
how can we combat the invisible

to remember here is to recall on purpose an awareness of the presence of God at our side
the names of God describe His attributes and powers, Father, Redeemer
Shepherd, Almighty
with all this alive in our hearts and minds there is a restoration of hope

be aware, this is no psychological trick to dislodge negative mind cycles
our union with the Lord is a real thing, our almighty Lord indwells us
He stills our fears as He stilled the waves[1]

this He has been doing, v56

the law is my song, recalled in the night, mentally, emotionally keeping close
darkness then revitalises my interest - it invigorates faith - it quickens life
and obedience follows naturally

the path to joy

as we align ourselves with Christ we attract attention - we can be sure that the forces of evil have our exact co-ordinates

vs51-52 we know ridicule and mockers, of being a joke and pathetic

vs53-54 we live in a world that has abandoned God and His laws, in conflict with the very laws we embrace

vs55-56 we experience the dark, feeling vulnerable and alone among invisible forces of good and evil

Zayin is about the formula for success as our faith is stress tested
that road testing outside in the real world, ... beyond church,
. . . . beyond personal devotions
Ephesians 6 is a NT parallel[2]
wrap me in Your love, give me protection - my shield of faith, my helmet of salvation, belt of truth etc

remember the tune of vs49-50

1. union with God is the source of all our strength and our salvation
begin to revel in Him and the nature of our relationship with Him

2. understanding this life we hold firm with a genuine sense of God's comfort and unison
1 Peter 4: 12-14[3] speaks of this and Christ who suffered Himself will surely uphold us

3. future proofed confidence happy that we can rely on Him
the future is secure - eternity is our home
through Christ we are now justified and cleansed from sin
we have opportunities while we lodge here to experience wonderful things

again
we have a living relationship with God . . .
we have a companion in this life to show us the way
we have our 119 guide that says this is the way
                    this is the path to eternal joy unspeakable

footnotes

1
Mark 4 : 38-41
But he was in the stern, asleep on the cushion. And they woke him and said to him, "Teacher, do you not care that we are perishing?" And he awoke and rebuked the wind and said to the sea, "Peace! Be still!" And the wind ceased, and there was a great calm. He said to them, "Why are you so afraid? Have you still no faith?" And they were filled with great fear and said to one another, "Who then is this, that even the wind and the sea obey him?"

2
Ephesians 6:10-17
. . . . Put on the whole armour of God, that you may be able to stand against the schemes of the devil. For we do not wrestle against flesh and blood, but against the rulers, against the authorities, against the cosmic powers over this present darkness, against the spiritual forces of evil in the heavenly places. Therefore take up the whole armour of God, that you may be able to withstand in the evil day, and having done all, to stand firm. Stand therefore, having fastened on the belt of truth, and having put on the breastplate of righteousness, and, as shoes for your feet, having put on the readiness given by the gospel of peace. In all circumstances take up the shield of faith, with which you can extinguish all the flaming darts of the evil one; and take the helmet of salvation, and the sword of the Spirit, which is the word of God,

3
1 Peter 4: 12-14
Beloved, do not be surprised at the fiery trial when it comes upon you to test you, as though something strange were happening to you. But rejoice insofar as you share Christ's sufferings, that you may also rejoice and be glad when his glory is revealed. If you are insulted for the name of Christ, you are blessed, because the Spirit of glory and of God rests upon you.

Heth

Psalm 119 : 57 - 64

The Lord is
my portion

Heth

57
The Lord is my portion;
I promise to keep your words.

58
I entreat your favour with all my heart;
be gracious to me according to your promise.

59
When I think on my ways,
I turn my feet to your testimonies;

60
I hasten and do not delay
to keep your commandments.

61
Though the cords of the wicked ensnare me,
I do not forget your law.

62
At midnight I rise to praise you,
because of your righteous rules.

63
I am a companion of all who fear you,
of those who keep your precepts.

64
The earth, O Lord, is full of your steadfast love;
teach me your statutes!

getting to know you

trip essentials

objective

speed

focus

lovingkindness

trip essentials

we move on from Zayin's stress test for faith and its triple formula for life
we are now more prepared to experience the unbelieving world
we learnt to remember that

       union with God is everything
       understanding life comes with embracing God's word
       future proofed confidence in heavenly joy

Zayin set out to give more clarity to the new faith orientated mindset
helping us to see our present time as it is, nested in eternity

Heth in turn will describe our ensuing deportment and behaviour
lots of action, lots of doing and with a sense of urgency
giving us a picture of what contemporary discipleship should look like day to day

while Zayin was best practice thinking - Heth is best practice doing

later 119 modules will progress through many facets of living the life
the attacks, the failures, the sorrows experienced in real time

but for now, what is our teacher's tip for today?
he says these four are the 'must have' things for the believer

objective   we need a target, where do we want to be?
vs57-58

speed   Paul spoke about running the race[1], no place for dawdlers (urgency)
vs59-60

focus   all departments working in harmony, facing the same way
vs61-62

lovingkindness   we must fill up on this one while in our dysfunctional world
vs63-64

objective

vs57-58
in a treasure hunt . . . we may well ask, what is the prize?
and with faith we ask, what's the point, is it worth the effort?

Heth shows us why it's worthwhile to mobilise body and mind
about the treasure that will set everything in motion?

the Lord is my portion . . v57
here we discover our ultimate treasure
everything we need for peace and joy is wrapped up in the Lord
He is our prime interest, the focus of all our resources
and be assured, this treasure deserves every ounce of our available effort

He is my portion: what actually is a portion? what is our Lord to us?
it means an allotment, as we understand an inheritance
> when we believe in the Lord we are adopted and thus in His family
it means a destiny, a lot or a share
> that remarkable awareness we have of Him, the attraction we feel
it means a dowry given to a bride
> the Lord is our bridegroom we are the bride . . His richness is ours

notice that getting to heaven is not mentioned
heaven is incidental, it happens to be where our Lord is
clearly, when we make the Lord our goal, heaven will follow

this *'portion'* word carries the notion of an intimate, personal engagement
so a harmony and union with Christ is our objective
> all actions in accord with our objective [1]
> this is what fixing eyes on Jesus [2] looks like

to love Him who first loved us [3] is to be embedded in our whole deportment

speed

vs59-60

when I think on my ways   -   I turn my feet to your testimonies
I hasten and do not delay   -   to keep your commandments

it's easy to be overwhelmed with personal administration
we have mail, emails, account statements, updates, feedbacks and bills
I wonder, do you have a method for dealing with it?
are you a 'last minute' person or do you have a clean desk policy?
so often, that which interests us most gets our attention first
. .we respond to bargain holiday offers quite quickly

in a way God also corresponds with us
He puts requests out to us in His Word that look for a response
it's like our administration in that we need to respond

we read in the Bible about
devotion, compassion, prayer, witness, tithing, patience, listening and so on
and will any of these crop up in our spiritual admin inbox
                              . . . has reading raised any action points?
just like secular admin . . action will relate to how much it interests us

keeping in mind the Lord is my portion, and its parallels with an inheritance
bridegrooms and destiny   . . . what is the response?

here in Heth, his response was - already sorted!
I have considered, I have done   I will hasten   I will not delay
our guide is no slacker, he is alive to his Lord and quick to respond

no place for procrastination
no danger of last minute   . . . . I'm going to, later . . . . .

but now we know the route to reform . . . .
when we make the Lord our portion and our focus we will surely see our spiritual
admin speeds increase dramatically

focus

vs61-62

though the cords of the wicked ensnare me, ... I do not forget your law.
at midnight I rise to praise you   ... because of your righteous rules

my neighbour can be seen on occasions adjusting his satellite dish
correct alignment is crucial for a good signal
even when the TV is off, the dish is aligned, ready, focused on the right satellite in the
sky

we are not expected to be in active holy contemplation all the time
we have trains to catch, reports to write, lessons to prepare, colours to choose.
but we are expected to always have correct alignment in our thinking
he gives two illustrations we can apply to our situations, snares and midnight

in the novel by Jonathan Swift, Gulliver, while not being attentive (asleep), finds
himself pegged down with many tiny threads and cannot move
for us, the real danger is allowing this life to take priority thread by thread and not
being awake

they may not have been literal cords in the Psalm
but rather the sense is the overwhelming influence of lesser attractions

the emphasis here is 'do not forget'   being actively mindful - this is post-it notes,
phone alerts or nudging each other
to actively keep your focus, watching for the gap that so easily opens up between us
and the Lord[4]

the emphasis here is 'to stay awake'   staying wakeful in appreciation, for Calvary,
new birth, for prayer
we can treat our redemption as we do terms and conditions, tick the box and
move on instead of being conscious of debt and active in our thanking

we know that using mobile phones while driving compromises focus on the
road ahead with increasing penalties
we cannot compromise our focus on our Lord
                         - the penalty for failure is unthinkable

lovingkindness

vs63-64
I am a companion to all who fear you, ... and all who keep your precepts.
the earth, O Lord is full of your steadfast love;   ..... teach me your statutes!

God is not soppy, He is not a pudding

God is strong, He is holy and to be seen with breathtaking awe
all this alongside His steadfast love
the world is full of His lovingkindness

let's dare to say .....
that God is overwhelmingly pleased with you as you turn toward Christ
that God maintains this planet in all its beauty and order as a gift to you and me
a token of His lovingkindness
we feast on His abundance

the church is still here against the odds
. . to nurture and advertise Christ's beauty and work

the Bible is His labour of love to enable you to absorb His loveliness
life is awash with His lovingkindness

as a new believer we 'gave our life to Christ'
that is the same as Your love is better than life in Psalm 63:3
the love of Christ is exquisite

we are invited to taste and see
shall we work on making the Lord our portion
looking for His face with all our being
because to fall into his arms is the ultimate bliss

footnotes

1

1 Corinthians 9:24-25
Do you not know that in a race all the runners run, but only one receives the prize? So run that you may obtain it. Every athlete exercises self-control in all things. They do it to receive a perishable wreath, but we an imperishable.

2
Hebrews 12:2
looking to Jesus, the founder and perfecter of our faith, who for the joy that was set before him endured the cross, despising the shame, and is seated at the right hand of the throne of God.

3
1 John 4:7-10
Beloved, let us love one another, for love is from God, and whoever loves has been born of God and knows God. Anyone who does not love does not know God, because God is love. In this the love of God was made manifest among us, that God sent his only Son into the world, so that we might live through him. In this is love, not that we have loved God but that he loved us and sent his Son to be the propitiation for our sins.

4
Hebrew 12 1-3
Therefore, since we are surrounded by so great a cloud of witnesses, let us also lay aside every weight, and sin which clings so closely, and let us run with endurance the race that is set before us, looking to Jesus, the founder and perfecter of our faith, who for the joy that was set before him endured the cross, despising the shame, and is seated at the right hand of the throne of God. Consider him who endured from sinners such hostility against himself, so that you may not grow weary or faint-hearted

Teth

Psalm 119 : 65 - 72

You are good
and you do good

Teth

65
You have dealt well with your servant,
O Lord, according to your word.

66
Teach me good judgement and knowledge,
for I believe in your commandments.

67
Before I was afflicted I went astray,
but now I keep your word.

68
You are good and do good;
teach me your statutes.

69
The insolent smear me with lies,
but with my whole heart I keep your precepts;

70
their heart is unfeeling like fat,
but I delight in your law.

71
It is good for me that I was afflicted,
that I might learn your statutes.

72
The law of your mouth is better to me
than thousands of gold and silver pieces.

putting on humility

the ideal

the ideal described

the ideal experienced

opposition to the ideal

embracing the ideal

the ideal

anyone who has adopted a dog that had been ill treated probably found it to be very suspicious at first, just because it had no previous experience of love

at first, we expect God to be like our experience of ourselves
God though, is not like us
we are goods damaged at the fall in Eden and He is always the impeccable God

we are encouraged to trust in this perfect being, God, but we tend to be suspicious of His intent and we reframe His kind suggestions with negativity

we are looking for the catch
we think the natural understanding we have from our previous experience is more trustworthy than the God revealed in the Bible

as we examine these verses monitor the scepticism at work in your mind
previous modules have established 'The Lord' as everything we need, past present and future, a universal solution

Teth, in a few lines, proposes an interface between us and this holy God,
we will probably ask, what does this unlikely coupling look like?

it is at once, simple and uncluttered   -   it's an **ideal** - the perfect situation for us to be in union with God

here we go, the **ideal** set out in four couplets
vs65-66 what is this **ideal** scheme?
vs67-68 a testimony by a newcomer who is just starting within the **ideal**
vs69-70 a look at problems that could occur within the **ideal**
vs71-72 the testimony-review of an experienced person within the **ideal**

the whole of 119 is moving steadily toward the problem of affliction
when the believer finds the unbelieving secular world overwhelming

Teth is about gaining spiritual strength, ready for such situations in the future

the ideal described

vs65-66

you have dealt well with your servant, O Lord, according to your word
teach me good judgement and knowledge, for I believe in your commandments

'good' appears four times in this module and the word can carry a variety of meanings, a 'good' child we imagine to be well behaved, obedient and a 'good' meal on the other hand would be beautifully prepared, flavoursome and very agreeable

when reading You are good, and what You do is good in v68 its sense will vary a lot depending on your meaning of the word 'good'
the three variations of the word 'good' used in Teth encompass agreeable, pleasant and joyful

the insolent translates inflated, bloated or puffed up in v69
the servant translates 'deflated' humble, bowed down in v65
here servant actually means servant
not as the social euphemism we see when signed as 'your obedient servant'

so far we have .... 'good' being delivered to the bowed down person on an industrial scale as promised by the infinite nature of God's Word

then in v66 the request is by the bowed down person
he asks for a beautiful combination of knowledge and good judgement

so our bowed down serf is much more than a 'Baldrick' with a swede for tea

when we recognise our true worth as a negative equity, we become eligible for God's bounty
while accepting pleasure, joy and satisfaction on a vast scale from our infinite Lord knowledge and fine judgement will be thrown in for good measure

we can have everything when we confess our sin before our dear Lord and relinquish that inflated opinion of self

the ideal experienced

before I was afflicted I went astray, but now I keep your word.
You are good and do good; teach me your statutes

throughout the Old Testament God is seen to bring affliction on people as a
corrective to bring them back into line with His Word
this was often a desperate last ditch necessity, when all else failed

but our ideal man sounds different
he describes his humbling as good, agreeable even pleasant
as is the God who humbles him
compared to 'going astray', the experience of being humbled was good

this experience of God being 'good' to him, prompts him to ask for more of it,
teach me more, having experienced it he wants to fill up on it

it is interesting to hear from one who was adjacent to both experiences saying
I was my own person … astray - now I'm humbled and emptied of arrogance
telling us that this detox of selfishness is a blast of pure joy, blowing in from the
Lord himself

now imagine the Lord being agreeable and delivering 'good' to you
what was experienced here is still available and recommended to us

would we dare ask sincerely that our beloved self sign up for such a detox, to
dump all that noxious gas of self possession and know it replaced by the beautiful
presence and joy of our Lord

now that is pretty well what this first hand review is asking of us
would we like to be converted from one way of operating as a person to a
completely different way, a way aligned to the person of Jesus Christ?

this would be a good thing
this would mean an agreeable, pleasant and a joyful thing

opposition to the ideal

vs69-70

The insolent smear me with lies, but with my whole heart I keep your precepts
their heart is unfeeling like fat, but I delight in your law

I said at the beginning we may be sceptical when we say that genuine humility
brings unexpected joy
..... it's probably a ploy to crush people after all - do the humble really experience
floods of joy?

maybe we are not going to all rush for the humble pie right now

yes - Teth is quite clear, the humbled do have a remarkable fellowship with God and
ensuing joy

Jesus Himself was deeply humbled as He laid aside His glory to undertake His
mission to redeem us on Calvary
that harrowing cry on the cross 'why forsaken' indicates the previously continuous
and happy union with His Father

the strongest opposition to being humble will be from natural arrogance within us
our internal pride will smear these ideas as half truths .... it's not really true

we are prone to a heart that is callous and unfeeling toward God v70
all around us is talk about asserting ourselves, empowerment and not much about
meekness and humility

Proverbs 3¹ says and James 4:6 quotes it - *God resists the proud and favours the*
humble and oppressed

Mary, as in Mary and Joseph, said *he has scattered the proud in the thoughts of*
their hearts; he has brought down the mighty from their thrones and exalted those
of humble estate; he has filled the hungry with good things, and the rich he has sent
away empty. Luke 1 : 51

embracing the ideal

vs71-72

It is good for me that I was afflicted, that I might learn your statutes.
The law of your mouth is better to me than thousands of gold and silver pieces

what then is learnt?
being humbled is better than having control over ourselves and our life

how would you come to that conclusion?
answer :
because to experience God's favour and goodness is *better* than all else by far

there is a difficulty though
if we have not experienced God's favour we may not come to that conclusion!
we'll stay with what we know

answer:
God's promises are true and found to be true by those who have tested them
the writer of Teth confirms to us it is so

our Lord asks us for commitment …for us to trust His words
v72 *'that I might learn your statutes'* …that we would put on humility

if we were to ask for some help here
perhaps God in His love to us would humble us
our inmost thoughts would be changed and we would know that embrace

when the noxious gas of pride is exhaled
we inhale the joy and beauty of Christ

to those who know because they trust
it's a no brainer

footnotes

1

Proverbs 3: 34-35
Towards the scorners he is scornful, but to
the humble he gives favour. The wise will
inherit honour, but fools get disgrace.

Yodh

Psalm 119 : 73 - 80

Let your steadfast
love comfort me

Yodh

73
Your hands have made and fashioned me;
give me understanding that I may learn your commandments.

74
Those who fear you shall see me and rejoice,
because I have hoped in your word.

75
I know, O Lord, that your rules are righteous,
and that in faithfulness you have afflicted me.

76
Let your steadfast love comfort me
according to your promise to your servant.

77
Let your mercy come to me, that I may live;
for your law is my delight.

78
Let the insolent be put to shame,
because they have wronged me with falsehood;
as for me, I will meditate on your precepts.

79
Let those who fear you turn to me,
that they may know your testimonies.

80
May my heart be blameless in your statutes,
that I may not be put to shame!

best love

introduction

early in 119 our man saw some people who were happy
blessed are those whose way is blameless, v1
who seek Him with their whole heart v2
. . . .and he went on through thick and thin to find that same joy and delight
he got to know God and to feel that relationship happening in real time

as he absorbs the words of God it translates into vital energy
he acquires skills and knowledge in a way that is valuable to any believer

this manual, so beautifully crafted in words and patterns continues to teach
us about walking with God in this life
these 22 modules of 'How to do it' Christian Living are designed to enthuse and
invigorate us

we have been encouraged to load up spiritual provisions and revised mindsets for
life when we are under attack
Yodh is one more package to tuck in our bag before the journey, a reference for
daily use on the journey ahead

1. we are *hand made* by God, this is remarkable v73

2. where affliction is infused with steadfast love vs75, 76, 77

3. the effects of witness in everyday life vs74, 78, 79

4. present attitude and future objectives v80

on being hand made

v73 begins with an immense statement couched in homely terms

things made by machine are by definition mechanical repetitions
while hand made objects are formed with thoughtfulness by an individual
such things carry the makers fingerprints, they're shaped according to their wish
this creative identity is why we keep the wobbly pots our children made

at some point we have made things ourselves and experienced the special affinity
we have with those things
therefore, we can understand in principle what God feels for us; His handiwork

your hands made me
we still carry His fingerprints in our individuality and we have a real connection to
the hand that made us as well as the mind that wanted us

what a denial to say we formed ourselves,
a rejection of the caring thoughts He had for us
was this triggered by a fear accountability [1] or claims a maker may have on us?

be amazed as God comes to calm our fears and to take us into His hands again
to restore that perfect relationship with Him
He is reunited with that which gave Him joy
like the woman in Luke 15 who said *rejoice with me, for I have found the coin that I
had lost*[2]

the sheer scale of this love for what His hand made is difficult for us to grasp
perfectly understandable is the request in *give me understanding to learn v73*

just what is it to be God's handiwork and reunited into His loving hands?

hand made faithfulness

faithfulness is not a soppy love v75
when our 'Maker' Father sees where we are now and where we need to be HE sets
the best course
God's utter truthfulness will apply **best practice** to obtain best result

notice: the couplet begins with an affirmation of trust
I know, O Lord, that your rules are righteous   I trust you altogether
this is a key attitude . . . . . that the Maker is greater than the object made

we are trusting that His words are good and right when our understanding fails!

unbelievers may not trust God or His words
resorting to a personal version of what is true and what to trust
but **God calls us** to be committed to **all** He says
to have complete trust in all His words

God's love may take us through hardship or affliction
but within this we *will see your steadfast love comfort us* v76
that affliction can be an opportunity for a display of faithful love that in other
situations we would not experience

our willingness to trust in affliction brings growth in understanding
our resentment to affliction can bring decline

be sure some affliction and disruption in our lives will occur on our journey

within such problems visible evidences of faithful love will be apparent to those
whose trust is completely fixed on God

hand made love and compassion

how we long to be understood and loved for who we are

Christ who made us and has walked this earth in flesh understands us
Christ who made us His child has unfailing love for us

because we ourselves cannot achieve steadfast love we have problems grasping the
immense promise *let your steadfast love comfort me v76*

as we kneel at His feet to receive His love
the comfort that accompanies His love is the evidence of it

Psalm 119 reminds us many times that trusting is about kneeling
about times in our own feebleness when we are overwhelmed with love

the word mercy or compassion v77 is care for the needy and the broken
the closer we come to Christ's beautiful thinking
the ugliness of ours becomes more apparent
He reaches out to restore us, to make us beautiful like Him
out of Him we are dead   -   in Him we live - just as v77 indicates

if we were dead and then made alive in Christ we would know it
when His Word becomes a delight . . . . . we will be conscious of delight

are we aware of
   Christ in our afflictions as evidence of faithful love
   kneeling before God and steadfast love bringing comfort
   His mercy coming to me as the gift of life

these elements stand us in good stead as we face the unbelieving world

the marks of hand made love

to see marks of God's love is good even when this visibility can be positive and
negative
we have three examples v74, v78 and v79

joy and rejoicing with other believers v74
hand made recipients of faithfulness, love and compassion will naturally meet with
joy because they have much in common, eternal hope - shared comfort and delight
our personal convictions are confirmed as we fellowship with other believers

loss of reputation v78
this is a temporary state of affairs
shame awaits the arrogant and proud
their negative action will still bring us confidence as we find comfort in recalling the
words of God's unfailing care for us

opportunities to share v79
being channels of God's mercy to others is another visible sign
compassion for the Lord's people is clearly spoken of by John in his epistle[3]
when people turn to us it can be a good opportunity to demonstrate God's
steadfast love as it flows through us

the last thought here is a reminder to be wholehearted v80
with the total display of God's faithfulness, love and compassion
we can experience the fellowship of the saints
how can we not be wholehearted?

footnotes

1
Isaiah 29:15-16
Ah, you who hide deep from the Lord your
counsel, whose deeds are in the dark, and
who say, "Who sees us? Who knows us?"
You turn things upside down!
Shall the potter be regarded as the clay,
that the thing made should say of its maker,
   "He did not make me";
or the thing formed say of him who
formed it,
   "He has no understanding"?

2
Luke 15:8-10
"Or what woman, having ten silver coins,
if she loses one coin, does not light a lamp
and sweep the house and seek diligently
until she finds it? And when she has
found it, she calls together her friends and
neighbours, saying, 'Rejoice with me, for I
have found the coin that I had lost.' Just so,
I tell you, there is joy before the angels of
God over one sinner who repents."

3
1 John 3:17
But if anyone has the world's goods and
sees his brother in need, yet closes his
heart against him, how does God's love
abide in him?

Kaph

Psalm 119 : 81 - 88

In your steadfast love
give me life

Kaph

81
My soul longs for your salvation;
I hope in your word.

82
My eyes long for your promise;
I ask, "When will you comfort me?"

83
For I have become like a wineskin in the smoke,
yet I have not forgotten your statutes.

84
How long must your servant endure?
When will you judge those who persecute me?

85
The insolent have dug pitfalls for me;
they do not live according to your law.

86
All your commandments are sure;
they persecute me with falsehood; help me!

87
They have almost made an end of me on earth,
but I have not forsaken your precepts.

88
In your steadfast love give me life,
that I may keep the testimonies of your mouth.

an anchor in heaven

time and eternity

anchors

information source

current devaluations

total trust

time and eternity

the apostle Paul, writing to the young Timothy said *all Scripture is breathed out by God and profitable for teaching, ... that the man of God may be competent, equipped for every good work*[1]   his words are direct and unequivocal putting the Bible at the centre of people and things

our world is largely in denial of such a profound phenomena

nevertheless, as we open the Bible we open a window into eternity
the words we read in time are a message from our timeless Maker
we ourselves are a mix of the finite body and the everlasting soul

God's Word has one foot in eternity and one foot on the earth. .... linking the finite and the infinite

as I think and move here in time, it is tracked in eternity
when God thinks and writes from eternity - do I recognise who is speaking?
believer or not, the connection is real ... even for sparrows[2]

in this module, Kaph recognises the validity of these connected zones
and writes as a man in time with his anchor in heaven
he is understanding life as informed by the eternal Word.

Kaph gives us a written message relating to real people
people grappling with the reality of two worlds and understanding how to behave
in a proper relationship with them both

anchors

the verses 81 - 88 are a half way point in this manual of life
here in a period of strife and trouble he calls out and nothing happens!
the line to eternity has gone dead
there is no relief from his troubles

look around .. is God and His Word in the news
is God on TV, or only as a parody?
around us we have sickness, blocked goals and little joy in a living Saviour

do we identify with Kaph
when will you comfort me? v82
how long must I endure? v84
help me! v86
they've almost made an end of me! v87
nevertheless our man still says his anchor is secure in heaven.
he says *I have not forsaken your precepts*

in previous modules he has been building up and storing provisions for these moments
these provisions are embedded in his thinking
whatever happens around him he will trust

read Kaph again and see   the silence
                                 the events
                                 the trust
                                 and the patience

until now we have mainly addressed the descriptive part of the couplet
we now look more at the responses
seeing those constant references to the Word, the living Word

information source

this direction of flow in his thinking is crucial
his engagement with 'the Word' informs him about his surroundings
while his surroundings do not influence his engagement with 'the Word'

there are moments when arm in arm with our Lord, we can see the futility of
world thinking - standing next to Christ, the world is seen for what it is, temporary,
rebellious and small minded

next day surrounded by media, society and pleasures …..doubt can creep in

is it really that black and white?
do I want room for some cultural compromise?

ask it again
which zone is your guide
        are we adjusting our understanding of Christ by social norms
        are we understanding social norms by 'the Word'
        which informs which

our man again and again displays his anchor - buried in the words of Christ
at every turn, every event, saying . . 'but I have not forsaken your precepts'
the life manual drives it home couplet after couplet - I'm safe and secure, wrapped
in the Word
they have almost made an end of me …. but I have not forsaken your precepts v87

observe the shrivelled bottle in the smoke, dried out in prolonged adversity and
endless trouble v83
still his anchor is in Christ
I have not forsaken your precepts v87

current devaluations

deception is a real danger
secret pitfalls for the unwary as the arrogant dig traps v85
persecuted, or direct social pressure with the backing of the establishment v86
they have almost made an end of me . . . . .actually killed, or at least killed my spirit to
own Christ v87

Jacques Derrida and his deconstruction theories build on Nietzsche's foundations
that in turn give us our postmodern thinking
his proposals that words are meaningless wrecks the foundation of trust and belief
. . . . in everything
'all words are an interpretation' there is no truth, period

the media now will cover an event and promptly swamp it with opinion, a myriad of
interpretations for you to wallow in
post-modernism's mantra is 'the only truth is that there is no truth'
like evolution this mantra is accepted everywhere

and when we proclaim a 'truth' we are laughed at or attacked
such as 86, when I say *all your commands are sure . . . . they persecute with falsehood*
any 'truth' in postmodern thinking is not only devalued it becomes a danger

we are also told God is a delusion, an idea to sweeten the reality of life
these ideas only exist in the confines of our minds
and if they colour the grey world for you, lucky you

our man is not so deluded
he is looking outside of himself

total trust

where it says *longs for* in v81 read patient longing for deliverance
longing, or love is joined to 'hope' as a certainty
this is so much more than ticking the 'I believe' box

then in v82 he moves higher, from the event to the promise.
moving from the gift to the giver
tranquillity in life may be denied
but he finds tranquillity **in his soul** as he rests in the Word

still nearer to the source he goes
In your steadfast love give me life,
that I may keep the testimonies of your mouth v88

all through time his anchor is firmly in Christ and His Word
we are encouraged to recognise the horrors of this world's thinking,
as we live among a vast array of tricks and traps, and the toxic thinking that we are
sprayed with every hour
- where is our anchor?

we must understand our surroundings by our grasp of the Word
not just the comprehension of our intellect
but a longing for the realisation of the living Word
or will we be duped into understanding God by world thinking?

remember Calvary as life and love pouring out
remember resurrection as our Jesus going ahead of us
who now looks for us to follow on . . . .

the prayer for our day is this prayer v88
in your steadfast love give me life
that I may keep your testimonies

footnotes

1
2 Timothy 3:16-17
All Scripture is breathed out by God and profitable for teaching, for reproof, for correction, and for training in righteousness, that the man of God may be competent, equipped for every good work.

2
Matthew 10 : 29-31
Are not two sparrows sold for a penny? And not one of them will fall to the ground apart from your Father. But even the hairs of your head are all numbered. Fear not, therefore; you are of more value than many sparrows.

Lamedh

Psalm 119 : 89 - 96

Forever, O Lord,
your word is firmly fixed
in the heavens

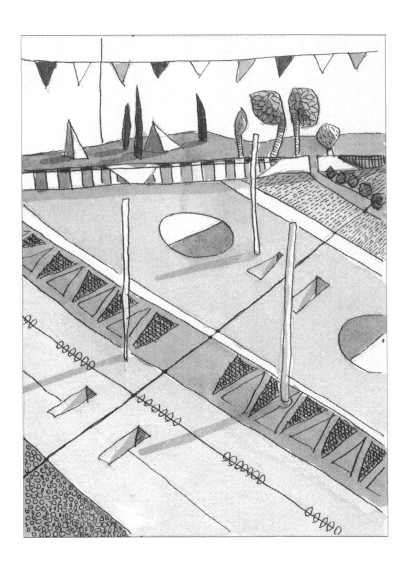

Lamedh

89
Forever, O Lord, your word
is firmly fixed in the heavens.

90
Your faithfulness endures to all generations;
you have established the earth, and it stands fast.

91
By your appointment they stand this day,
for all things are your servants.

92
If your law had not been my delight,
I would have perished in my affliction.

93
I will never forget your precepts,
for by them you have given me life.

94
I am yours; save me,
for I have sought your precepts.

95
The wicked lie in wait to destroy me,
but I consider your testimonies.

96
I have seen a limit to all perfection,
but your commandment is exceedingly broad.

close up with God

eight statements

coloured thinking

re-appraisal

personification

upscaling 'Jesus'

eight statements

in Kaph we saw our man weathering a personal storm with his anchor firmly grounded in God's words
he was understanding the prevailing standards from this heavenly standpoint …
and not modifying his opinion of God according to social pressure

if Kaph was an action module, Lamedh is the calculation behind the action
in Lamedh there are no questions, only statements
these eight lines are eight statements governing the interplay between heaven and earth
no small thing!

God's throne is beyond time, it is immutable and constant v89

God is interested in us - His handiwork is consistent and immovable v90

everything is in place because He says so, and everything obeys Him v91

my relationship with Your rules relieves my difficult situation v92

God's gift to me of life keeps His words alive in me v93

in Your rules, I discover I am Yours and I have a need v94

in spite of threats my focus is on God's words v95

my experience is limited: while God's scope is unlimited v96

these eight statements make up Lamedh

coloured thinking

grasping the scale and the nature of God can stretch our finite mindsets
the medieval sound of this deity may well hinder our enthusiasm for Him
we have to ask if our integration in modern life will subconsciously restrict our
willingness to 'delight' in these declarations?

perhaps we find the person of Jesus an easier package to relate to when we
visualise Him as a wandering underdog confounding the establishment with His nifty
arguments
or perhaps a Jesus as the original 'superman' who single handed saves the world
while having the time to speak to children and heal the sick

we may find these Lamedh statements uncompromising, statements that
ring alarm bells in our head as we recall totalitarian governments, corporate
overreach or any of those systems that seek world domination

for instance when speaking about *all things* in v91
by your appointment they stand this day, for all things are your servants
does this delight you or frighten you . . . does it suggest a loss of identity?
does it liberate or suffocate?

our man in v92 is delighted with the idea of the almighty God having the credit for
everything
if your law had not been my delight I would have perished in my affliction

can we join his enthusiasm and delight in this package or has our thinking been
coloured over the years making this a step too far for us?

re-appraisal

let's review our mindset
remember that an environment where 'Bible as truth' is not accepted is a difficult
place for us to recognise the beauty of God Almighty

making gods suit our own requirements is a popular way to satisfy our spiritual
needs,
a god that we can 'manage'
but our thinking is infected by the delusion that we can be masters of our own
destiny
we are re-modelling the infinite God on finite understanding

but what if our thinking is infected by the delusion that we can be masters of our
own destiny
and that the relinquishing of identity and freedom can sound so wrong

but what if Lamedh shows us God is total beauty, total joy, endless delight and
justice   ...... could we be persuaded?

Lamedh presents an eternal, immutable being v89
Lamedh presents universal obedience by everything v91
Lamedh presents rescue and subsequent belonging v94

is this a delight?

if the beauty of Christ is summed up in Lamedh .... would you marry Him?

to the modern mind, Lamedh is formidable material
shall we insist on remodelling perfection, modelling a god to accommodate our
limited understanding v96

or shall we marry the Prince, then relish His beauty and His glory

personification

aware that we may be hesitant, we are reminded of two things
God's Word is rock solid in eternity as well as here in time v89
God's faithfulness to us is observed as continuous through all generations v90
we are given a reminder of God's pedigree

Jesus, as a figure we quite like and on the whole identify with
among other things His coming was to show Himself to us as understandable within
the limitations of time and space
and to show the ideal relationship He enjoyed with His Father

we note that the actions and status of Jesus Christ as described in ch1 of John's
gospel are in a similar vein to the God in v89
this Jesus is God and infused with all the qualities of God
they are of one mind, a communion in prayer abounds
Jesus loves to do the Father's will and so on
everything He does is to communicate to us the faithful love of God
this same God we find in Lamedh

if the Lord Jesus embraces everything about His Father
how can we remodel any part of His written Word
he is both lovely and awesome

upscaling 'Jesus'

I'm encouraging us to see our 'Jesus' and the grand Lamedh vision as one,
to upscale 'our little' Jesus to embody the idea of that all embracing God
He is the voice that we can identify with, as well as the One who reveals Almighty
God to us

we have the One who said '*let the little children come to me*,' Matthew 19:14[2]
being the same One who stands in heaven
He who said to the waves *be still* [3]
is the same One whose laws endure, all things serve you! in v91

that good shepherd who comes to find us also makes an appearance in Lamedh in
v94 *I am yours, save me*

you are looking at the heart of Him who *made everything and who is served by
everything* v91
who has been faithful in His redeeming mission through all generations v90
Lamedh is big Jesus . . . . *I am yours, save me!* v94

Lamedh would be terrifying if it was anyone but Jesus . . . full of grace and truth
let's turn away from the bleakness of our past - where we would perish in afflictions
it's time to revise our thinking
kiss the Son in faith. . . make His law your delight v92

previously we saw a man able to endure the trials of life because his anchor was in
heaven
this Jesus is the personification of heaven
with our anchor in Christ we can indeed smile at any storm

footnotes

1
John 1:1-5
In the beginning was the Word, and the Word was with God, and the Word was God. He was in the beginning with God. All things were made through him, and without him was not any thing made that was made. In him was life,[a] and the life was the light of men. The light shines in the darkness, and the darkness has not overcome it.

2
Matthew 19:14
but Jesus said, "Let the little children come to me and do not hinder them, for to such belongs the kingdom of heaven."

3
Mark 4:38-40
But he was in the stern, asleep on the cushion. And they woke him and said to him, "Teacher, do you not care that we are perishing?" And he awoke and rebuked the wind and said to the sea, "Peace! Be still!" And the wind ceased, and there was a great calm. He said to them, "Why are you so afraid? Have you still no faith?"

Mem

Psalm 119 : 97 - 104

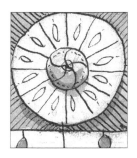

How sweet are
your words to my taste,
sweeter than honey
to my mouth!

134   getting to know God

Mem

97
Oh how I love your law!
It is my meditation all the day.

98
Your commandment makes me wiser than my enemies,
for it is ever with me.

99
I have more understanding than all my teachers,
for your testimonies are my meditation.

100
I understand more than the aged,
for I keep your precepts.

101
I hold back my feet from every evil way,
in order to keep your word.

102
I do not turn aside from your rules,
for you have taught me.

103
How sweet are your words to my taste,
sweeter than honey to my mouth!

104
Through your precepts I get understanding;
therefore I hate every false way.

loves animating power

assembling the parts

love as an energy source

the route to understanding

words that set me in motion

accord

assembling the parts

when we attend church, we call it worship
there we sing God's praise in song

keep the word 'worship' in mind but uncouple it from church and God
when the word is applied person to person, it becomes 'he worships her,'
or 'she adores him,' and maybe 'he is forever singing her praises'
with God the word 'worship' adopts a more formal, almost stilted usage while with
people it is more animated

how do we read v97 *Oh how I love your law! it is my meditation all the day*
like our use of the word 'worship', do we re-imagine our idea of 'love' when relating
it to God?
in this context, does love really have 'animating power'?[1]

in this module we find

v97 first we meet love, as an energising passion, motivating him all day
vs98-100 secondly, God given understanding is presented three ways; regarding it
better than his enemies, teachers and elders
vs101-102 thirdly, he records action that results in life changing applications

a remarkable parallel is found in Philippians 2: 12-13 *Therefore, my beloved, as you
have always obeyed, so now, not only as in my presence but much more in my absence,
work out your own salvation with fear and trembling, for it is God who works in you, both
to will and to work for his good pleasure.*
as it tracks love, devotion to Christ, understanding, humility and the exhortation to
work out our salvation with fear and trembling
simplified they could be   HEAT : the love of our heart.
                                LIGHT : the understanding of our mind
                                POWER : the action of our will

'Mem' and Philippians seek to synchronise our parts
                          to a common end - a christian life
when heart, mind and will are together what can we not achieve?
would we not expect God of all people to bring such harmony to the born again
believer!

love as an energy source

while God is always trying to draw us toward a greater harmony of being
the old nature is always against it
throughout history we see examples of relapse and compromise
there is a continual reticence for people to engage with God in love

we know that love has animating power, an exciting energy
while indifference is joined to apathy
the encouragement to love God is well rehearsed in christian rhetoric
but where do we look for a suitable reservoir to draw from
little is to be found within ourselves, our bias is for less christian things

our man applies to the best and inexhaustible reservoir - God Himself
v41 *Let your steadfast love come to me, that I may live and keep your word*
unlike our resources this love is steadfast, dependable and faithful
and available for the asking

the Psalm sets out a destination
God is to be our centre and thus a harmony for our being
ask me He says and I will provide the engine to take you there
this is the love that I can give you
by v97, he seems to have arrived and is motivated to love and meditate all day

while this may seem somewhat airy fairy and other worldly
Paul in Philippians is firmly grounded
ch1:19-20 Eager expectation - through your prayers and the help of the Holy Spirit
ch1:21 for me to live is Christ, to die is gain

this is real life, not airy fairy

the route to understanding

like many enclaves of knowledge
the Renaissance and the Enlightenment celebrated humanism and sought to make
'man' the measure of all things

not unlike today when **my enemies** v98
are set up by the enemy of our souls with fake truths and fake promises
we must spot the spoof or the spam .... we need to be wiser than them

we read of **teachers** v99
secular studies and awards abound, promising to take us higher up the ladder
there are academic skills, the learning of the past and new learning of today
much that will fail us when we consider what the soul needs now
and will fail us at the judgement after death

generations past - parental and social influence v100
like media and advertising feeding material to our minds
all the current understanding of how to live
but still with man as the measure of all things

only God's Word prepares the soul for eternity

God's Word, is not too fantastic to believe, He is to be
        the love of our hearts
        the understanding of our minds
        the action of our will

we can be aided and activated by love when we ask for an infusion of love!
let your love come to me v41
You God (Your words) are sweeter than honey to my mouth
honey is likened to the realities of love v103
in those pre sugar days honey was pure bliss.
God, Your words are pure bliss to me

words that set me in motion

we have been fed lies and delusions - by Satan
self is a poor judge of genuine joy
while fake things can easily entertain us

perhaps the word lethargy could describe our efforts to engage with God
joined with displacement activity, delay or cancellation will follow

what can break the mould?

Christ is the most beautiful, most indulgent, most *honey in the mouth* destination in
the world
dare to believe that, dare to ditch 'the agenda of self' and 'the wish list of want'
kneel as a misguided spiritual layabout and ask God that His love would come to
you, to fill and overflow you

just for now, forget debates of doctrinal niceties and dry histories

His words are not academic, ... they are sweet *honey in the mouth* words,
we begin to have 'greedy for God' moments
like *Oh how I love your law - It is my meditation all the day* v97

loves animating power is where delight delivers understanding
and understanding converts to motion

I hold back my feet from every evil way,
      in order to keep your word v101
Through your precepts I get understanding;
      therefore I hate every false way v104

accord

the apostle Paul said *complete my joy by being of the same mind, having the same love, being in full accord and of one mind, Do nothing from rivalry or conceit, but in humility count others more significant than yourselves* Phil 2: 2-3
he is saying embrace the everyday Christ

the message of Mem is for everyone's everyday living
the theme is accord
Paul enthuses us to follow the Mem way
same love (from God) same mind (understanding) do nothing for self

I remind you where we began .. to synchronise our parts to one purpose
there will be a conflict with our old nature to the very end
but no reason to sleep with the enemy now
so, throw caution to the wind
ask God to pour his steadfast love into our hearts

can we be enthused
as this Psalm enthuses us to take a step forward in spiritual life
                        .... alone we are wimps, we will lose before we start
only when we reach out to Jesus Christ for HIS steadfast love can we hope to leave
this lethargy behind

Philip Doddridge hymn writing in the 18th century penned the lines
'Tis to my Saviour I would live
His love hath animating power

this is a message of profound love, for everyone, for the everyday
it is for the asking

footnotes

1
a quote from the 18th century hymn
writer Philip Doddridge's hymn
'My gracious Lord I own the right'

v4
But to my Saviour I would live,
to him who for my ransom died;
nor could untainted Eden give
such bliss as blossoms at his side.

v5
His work my later tears shall bless,
when youthful vigour is no more,
and my last hour of life confess
his love hath animating pow'r.

walking with God

Nun

Psalm 119 : 105 - 112

... a light to
my path

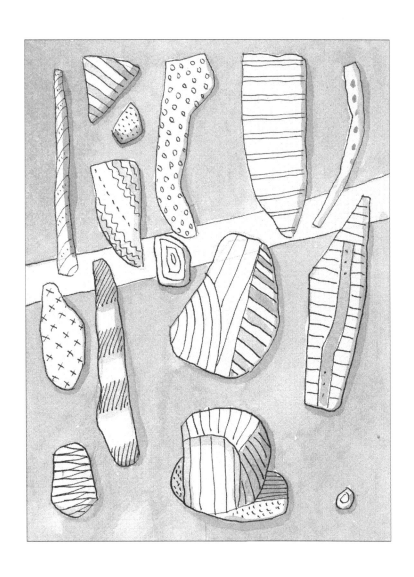

Nun

105
Your word is a lamp to my feet
and a light to my path.

106
I have sworn an oath and confirmed it,
to keep your righteous rules.

107
I am severely afflicted;
give me life, O Lord, according to your word!

108
Accept my freewill offerings of praise, O Lord,
and teach me your rules.

109
I hold my life in my hand continually,
but I do not forget your law.

110
The wicked have laid a snare for me,
but I do not stray from your precepts.

111
Your testimonies are my heritage for ever,
for they are the joy of my heart.

112
I incline my heart to perform your statutes
for ever, to the end.

a light to my path

the path

the nature of the path

singing on the path

the dangers on the path

happy on the path

the path

we ended Mem with Philip Doddridge's lines about *loves animating power*
a love that works as an injection of energy

animated in what way?
hyper activity can be random multi-directional and undisciplined
love can go round in obsessive self absorbed circles

this module speaks of the path we are to take
the narrow linear path that leads to everlasting life
Matthew 7 reflects on the path metaphor saying it is a hard path[1] that will sap our
energies but we can be sure that the reservoir of God's love can be tapped for its
animating power

it's also a path in the darkness (of sin) else why would a lamp be needed
the 18th century thought it was the age of enlightenment while in fact it was
spreading the darkness of humanism, making a path in accord with our natural sin
bias that excludes God

the phrases *to keep* v106 *not stray from* v110 hint at a tendency to stray

those crossing the Maplin sands on the dangerous Broomyard path will see the way
marked with tall sticks to keep the travellers safe on that deadly expanse of sand
happily God's Word defines a path for us as we travel through the dangers that
stand between us and life eternal

the promise to follow in v106 adds genuine focus to life and an awareness of our
own fickleness
even with the power of God's love on tap and the understanding we have on board
the promise to ACT is needed
for us to actually step out on the path is so important

the nature of the path

for us God Himself indicates the best (only) route
according to your word, v107 is prescribed as our guiding light
keeping His decrees to the very end
all the while we're checking the validity of choices and actions by the book
earlier we found that God's Word merges with our understanding
and understanding is as much a gift as the book itself

many people want to understand the universe with their own intellect
here the writer surrenders any such claim and asks for divine enlightenment
this is the hard bit, surrendering!
when we believe and trust is when we walk on water

our new path tends not to follow contours or avoid obstacles and difficulties, rather
it meets things head on
as we read Nun it's more like following a compass bearing in a forest.
I will walk in this prescribed direction regardless of obstacles
it's a mix of willing praise, heritage and joy along with suffering and snares

there is rigour here, strictness with self to abide by the righteous rules v106
remember Paul and his race illustrations when he had made a commitment that
caused him to lay aside every weight that would restrict him
so similar to our module here - I will follow, .. not forget, ... my oath
see his post-it note reminders to self in v106, mentally scrolling through the
requirements

it leads him to
life eternal, the love of his life, profound value, the joy of his heart v111

Paul again says, run as to win the prize, run with every ounce of energy
drawing on loves animating power
the path is not a picnic, it's the path that will take us to the picnic

singing on the path

earlier we spoke of Heat/love - Light/understanding - Power/actions
God bringing us to this place of synergy, to a harmony of purpose
when we are born again and give ourselves to God
where doing is infused with divine love and understanding

while this new life is informed and empowered by God
it is tested in the mud and grit of day to day living
our man encourages us to be committed and follow in obedience
as we may have sung -   O Jesus I have promised
                           to serve thee to the end

it reveals the overriding of self and contrition of our heart
with our voice in v108
with our hands in v109
these externalise the new thinking and the new willing - aka commitment
willingness is very acceptable to God

not a fleeting whim but my heritage for ever v111
I take my life in my hands and place it in God's care and wisdom v109
visualise :- permanence, being steadfast, to have made up my mind[2]
these solid joys are best

here the joy in the heart overflows in the praises of the mouth
it can be that the act of singing itself can cheer us
and when with other singing people we can be encouraged

but this is different in v108 we find the opposite direction of travel
here the effect is like a fountain of internal joy that must praise in song
it carries the authenticity of its internal source
as opposed to more intermittent external effects

your testimonies are my heritage forever
for they are the joy of my heart v111

the dangers on the path

I have suffered much v107 as a result of following the path
on the way that leads to eternal joy there will be hardship and pain
we read *the narrow way is hard* in Matthew ch7[1]
but we can have our energy delivered by His love . . . for we are in Christ's care.

the promise to galvanise, made because he was not aware of difficulties
David had physical and political dangers
while ours are more social, more behavioural and a different kind of wounding
will we make the act of setting a course and sticking to it a priority

it is conscious risk taking, taking my life in my hands v109
pro actively like Peter,[3] stepping out of the safety of the boat to be among the
waves with his eyes on Jesus
called to live dangerously. risking Satan's ambushes
remembering Joshua's hornets that went in front[4] Joshua 24:12

the crafty poacher will set snares in a 'run' or path
and the enemy of souls will camouflage snares in our path v110
IED's (improvised exploding device) in modern warfare are set beside the road
we in modern spiritual warfare risk equal dangers on our path
despite the dangers .. we must keep on the path or we will not arrive

we need that light to see the path . . . .and to understand
after all, my understanding now confirms the path is right
there is accord as I praise You while I walk v108
and the path however hard is praised willingly
happily keeping to the path
keeping the decrees to the very end

happy on the path

that agreement of heart, will and mind is a lovely synergy
Francis Chichester used a sextant while on his boat taking regular bearings from the
sun to calculate his position
then using his charts and all his navigational skills
he came at last to his destination

His Word is a light for us, being devoted and obedient to our Lord
v I I I reveals our joy in the objective
bliss is both present joy and anticipation
my mind is set on keeping Your Word
I'm concentrating, I'm intentional
it is not left to luck

on one famous path to Emmaus two men walked with Jesus,[5]
they had the greatest teacher ever to explain the Bible to them
recalling the incident later they said *did not our hearts to burn within us*
their experience was that God can really infuse us with His Spirit
not in a fleeting way … but to the end

with this living union with Christ
born again with the witness of His Spirit living within us
we wish for no compromise in our path … now lit up by His Word

our hearts are full, so happy in our living Lord
our hearts are set on keeping your Word that is our path
I can know this to be the joy of my heart .. to the very end

footnotes

1
Matthew 7: 13-14
"Enter by the narrow gate. For the gate is wide and the way is easy that leads to destruction, and those who enter by it are many. For the gate is narrow and the way is hard that leads to life, and those who find it are few.

2
James 1:6
But let him ask in faith, with no doubting, for the one who doubts is like a wave of the sea that is driven and tossed by the wind.

3
Matthew 14 : 28-31
Peter answered him, "Lord, if it is you, command me to come to you on the water." He said, "Come." So Peter got out of the boat and walked on the water and came to Jesus. But when he saw the wind, he was afraid, and beginning to sink he cried out, "Lord, save me." Jesus immediately reached out his hand and took hold of him, saying to him, "O you of little faith, why did you doubt?"

4
Joshua 24 :12-13
And I sent the hornet before you, which drove them (the enemy) out before you, the two kings of the Amorites; it was not by your sword or by your bow. I gave you a land on which you had not laboured and cities that you had not built, and you dwell in them. You eat the fruit of vineyards and olive orchards that you did not plant.'

5
Luke 24 : 29-32
When he was at table with them, he took the bread and blessed and broke it and gave it to them. And their eyes were opened, and they recognized him. And he vanished from their sight. They said to each other, "Did not our hearts burn within us while he talked to us on the road, while he opened to us the Scriptures?"

Samekh

Psalm 119 : 113 - 120

Hold me up,
that I may be safe

Samekh

113
I hate the double-minded,
but I love your law.

114
You are my hiding place and my shield;
I hope in your word.

115
Depart from me, you evildoers,
that I may keep the commandments of my God.

116
Uphold me according to your promise, that I may live,
and let me not be put to shame in my hope!

117
Hold me up, that I may be safe
and have regard for your statutes continually!

118
You spurn all who go astray from your statutes,
for their cunning is in vain.

119
All the wicked of the earth you discard like dross,
therefore I love your testimonies.

120
My flesh trembles for fear of you,
and I am afraid of your judgements.

hold me up

tactical thinking

God Almighty

smart moves

self assessment

wake up call

tactical thinking

so far
the pathway to life has been discovered and described as narrow and hard
there is a lamp and light to guide our feet
even where there is danger there is also joy and singing in prospect
this is no ordinary path

our guide knows the path, he is a committed path user and lays out a plan for us
from data he has gathered from experience
Nun was his assessment of the situation, short but comprehensive
practical notes on How to Live forever

it is an organised plan of personal commitment
a way to be steadfast and embrace single mindedness

from Aleph we remember being half hearted
now is time for a pause, a time for careful thought
the module is about tactical thinking
having become sensitive to weakness and instability

what issues are we dealing with and what material are we working with?
with me is the most awesome being ever contemplated, God Almighty
and all the while there is heavy incoming fire from the dark side
some being obvious and some concealed within very clever camouflage

these 16 lines are good advice for the path from here to eternity
the Bible may be old, but when read - its beauty is contemporary
this material is not for sticky post-it notes
these notes should be etched into the fridge door itself

God Almighty

God says *I am the first and I am last*[1] without doubt the greatest player on the stage
as such we are bound to consider and revere Him
God says He is our beginning and our end
when should we consider this, now or when we are introduced?
much better to think about Him now

like it or not He is woven in to everything and in to every couplet in this Psalm
His Word is a manifest of Himself
we are not holding a holy brochure here
nor is it a pitch by God, giving us the opportunity to consider alternatives
the Bible is a big reveal, a declaration of how things are

God is awesome as v120 indicates
but then think of all the evil in this world, the visible powers of darkness
what champion will grasp the collar of that monster and put things to right?
looking around me today, I so want an awesome God

God demands attention - His Word of truth is still in print
earth defies comprehension, revealing ever more complex layers
 .. and still His hand is proffered
          come to me, all who labour ... I will give you rest[2]

everything about God is vast, His love, His rewards, His power to keep
how profound to be softly wrapped in Him as a refuge, wrapped within a shield of
His making v114
happy to know my future is entrusted to the truth of His Word

smart moves

we can all recall embarrassing moments
the disciples were caught asleep in Gethsemane, unable to watch for an hour!
we all have 'stray' moments or perhaps 'stray from path' whole afternoons
fortunately they are not recorded in the Bible
so when we read I hate double-mindedness v113 we need to pay attention!

our writer is really smart here
knowing his own failure rate - he installs some path failure alarms
after all he does have a historic problem *Oh that my ways may be steadfast.* v5
now why would he say that?
could v113 be about himself and for himself?
> I hate myself having faith failures .. but I love loving your law

away from me evildoers v115
lay alongside this Jesus saying *if your eye causes you to sin, tear it out.* !3
meaning that if parts of us distract or weaken focus, 'away' with them
like the offending eye, it is hyperbole, but with message
ban anything that distracts me from keeping Your Word as well as I can for my Jesus

be aware of the real danger of self delusions
be sure that any age or epoch will have its own fake paths
being tricked into fake paths is possible and carries the danger of rejection v118
check bearings, check relationship to the cross and to our Saviour

see the discarded ones v119, and avoid the pitfall by active love
look and learn, stay smart

these are not pathetic sanctimonious clichés   soppy Sunday stuff
these are best eternal life skills
these are hard-nosed 'way to heaven' markers

for us

self assessment

while we now have the necessary wit to proceed . . . . do we have the ability?
our writer friend and guide identifies two areas likely to be lacking
they are - lack of shielding and lack of adequate strength
without addressing these there is no execution of the plan

asking for help is a major recurring theme in 119, *hold me up* v117
cyber security is bad enough to get right
but spiritual security on the path is high risk
we are always exposed to the enemy of souls
beware: invisible risks are easily dismissed and inertia reigns

security is *my shield* v114 we must not underestimate the dangers of being duped
and deluded
an attack is unlikely to be obvious
like a satanic messenger hunting believers at the front door
it's going to be sneaky, a sleepy gas sort of thing
we need top end Holy Spirit protection against an unseen enemy

uphold me v116 a genuine call from someone unable to manage his own life
after a hard look at his personal track record he is genuinely frightened at his own
lack of ability to keep on the path
the recommendation is, be smart, wake up to our human spiritual feebleness

hold me up v117 a genuine call from someone who recognises their inability to hold
their own in the spiritual war
protect from delusions of my own imagined power and ability
and a misjudgement of enemy intent

Matthew 6:13. *Deliver us from evil* [4] and here . . .I shall be delivered

wake up call

it's a time for awe v120 when maybe we're in snooze mode
God is not impressed with inertia
we are exposed to dangers here and He fears for us
keep on the path
faith is not recreational! not a week-end event when time allows
it's a matter of eternal life or everlasting death

see the move from delusion to clarity in vs118-120
see the near miss of one who 'strays'
see the effect of the indulgence of a foot in each camp

let's ask God for a grasp of the gravity of the situation that we are assessing
begin to hate double mindedness v113
oust any twin agendas - two masters - half heartedness - lukewarmness
remember faith is not a recreational aside, it's the path to life

then love His law v113 seek out loves animating power
for His love for us knows no bounds
the blood of Christ at Calvary is the proof of that
He wants us home with Him
think of Him as jumping up and down to wake us up

Samekh says - eternal life is not a given, we need to think and act.
Samekh says - look at your track record, we will need some help here
Samekh says - God you are my everything
        be smart, active and intelligent
        ask God for help
        wrap yourself in His righteousness

footnotes

1

Isaiah 44: 6
Thus says the Lord, the King of Israel
    and his Redeemer, the Lord of hosts:
"I am the first and I am the last;
    besides me there is no god.

2

Matthew 11 : 28-29
Come to me, all who labour and are heavy
laden, and I will give you rest. Take my yoke
upon you, and learn from me, for I am
gentle and lowly in heart, and you will find
rest for your souls

3

Mark 9:47
And if your eye causes you to sin, tear
it out. It is better for you to enter the
kingdom of God with one eye than with
two eyes to be thrown into hell

4

Matthew 6:13 (the Lords prayer)
And lead us not into temptation,
    but deliver us from evil.

Ayin

Psalm 119 : 121 - 128

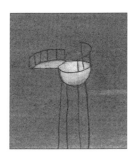

I love your
commandments
above gold,
above fine gold

Ayin

121
I have done what is just and right;
do not leave me to my oppressors.

122
Give your servant a pledge of good;
let not the insolent oppress me.

123
My eyes long for your salvation
and for the fulfilment of your righteous promise.

124
Deal with your servant according to your steadfast love,
and teach me your statutes.

125
I am your servant; give me understanding,
that I may know your testimonies!

126
It is time for the Lord to act,
for your law has been broken.

127
Therefore I love your commandments
above gold, above fine gold.

128
Therefore I consider all your precepts to be right;
I hate every false way.

exhilarating joy

faith as a bungee jump

watch my back

future proof

moved by love

the love of your life

faith as a bungee jump

the self assessment in Samekh looked at weaknesses and solutions
he was beefing up his confidence with clear tactical thinking
gathering in any loose ends that may impede his progress on the path

now the rigours of this path to life do expose us to emotional damage
Bible belief in the 21st century is a wrecker of social reputations
hold me up he says in v117… I really want to do the right thing

back in v120 he has a bit of a melt down
I am shaking with fear - You are awesome

there he is frightened to jump and frightened not to
like the prospect of death or exhilarating joy in a bungee jump

In Ayin he steps up to the line
ready to take God at His word[1]

quietly he formulates three requests
  please, watch my back in the danger zones
  please, fulfil Your promise to me
  please, give me an understanding of values

and then he sums up his reasons to proceed
he loves holiness more than sin
it seems like a work of grace has taken place in his heart
  he loves God more than himself and anything he has

watch my back

when I take the plunge … please keep me safe vs121-122
safe from what? ….what is the danger here
how will an oppressor oppress?
the Hebrew word 'oppress' has its root in violation and deception
not so much of the body, more a violation of our holiness
a sort of spiritual rape
these arrogant ones are those who will not kneel to Christ
and not able to spoil Christ himself, they seek to spoil us instead

Philippians 3:17-20 …. keep your eyes on those who walk according to the example
you have in us. For many, of whom I have often told you and now tell you even with tears,
walk as enemies of the cross of Christ. Their end is destruction, their god is their belly and
they glory in their shame, with minds set on earthly things
but our citizenship is in heaven

you see how valid his fear is, how easily we are led astray
our goal to be like Christ is easily tarnished
not unlike a paintball battle, where you work toward a target zone, to arrive without
being splattered by the opposition
I see a parallel here
how alert, and cautious we would be if spiritual life was as visual as paintballing

he is aware that protection is needed
his smart move was to call for divine help
please ensure my well being - do not leave me to my own devices vs121-122
listen to Jude as he acknowledges God in his prayer for others in v24:
Now to him who is able to keep you from stumbling and to present you blameless
before the presence of his glory with great joy
it's God who can keep us and present us blameless
how vulnerable do we see ourselves?

future proof

with dangers dealt with, the request now is about seeing ahead
I so want to see the reward, I long for heaven! v123
and, deal with me according to Your wonderful attribute of love v124
this is reminiscent of v41, *let your steadfast love come to me*

we may look at holiday brochures and long for a holiday
but to go on holiday we have to pick up the phone and make the booking
we have to commit

we need to plead *deal with your servant according to your steadfast love v124*
in New Testament language it's you and me kneeling at the cross of Christ
this is the place we can 'see' the love of Christ as it is delivered to us
this is where our personal compounded sin is separated from us
and annihilated

just interest in salvation is not enough, we have to commit
kneeling at the cross is the entrance to 'the Way', it is the gateway to heaven

many saw Christ die at Calvary and did not see what was really happening
we can sing the words of 'Amazing Grace' - and see a song lyric without the reality
and the wonder of our sin being dealt with by grace

as we follow the module through we detect a growing confidence
a love that progresses to action

here our soul is future proofed
here I start understanding the work of grace at Calvary
here is perfect peace and every guilt removed

moved by love

now v126 is a bold move!
to say 'it is time for you to act; your law is being broken'
who would dare to call down a holy God's judgements on a fallen world
only someone who is convinced of salvation and knows sin forgiven

then in vs127-128
there is progression to positive delight and obedience - I have done this!
there is real devotion to God and His words, I love them, I long for them
how beautiful is willingness that flows from love .... compared to duty

v127 *love ... above gold, above fine gold*
we know how gold is loved and valued by people
but now we are navigating to a realm beyond this popular metal
where earthly values turn to dust
his heart, his love is entwined with the words of the One he loves
these words contain a truth that overturns the power of death
and ushers us into a realm of peace and perfection

this is the big one
will we trade what we have for what we are promised in God's Word

or as Jesus would later say in Matthew 16: 24-25 ... *if anyone would come after me, let him deny himself and take up his cross and follow me. For whoever would save his life will lose it, but whoever loses his life for my sake will find it.*

the love of your life

because of love, v127, because it's right, v128, …I do this and this
we hear it from him again and again
Your love has animating power
love prevents me from straying from the path

let's be reminded about some elements of the path
of the dangers, please save me from oppressors who may violate me
this path is a spiritual path - I may be strange to other people
please come close to me Lord so I will see and understand this path

the default heart we all start with needs a revolution
it needs God's hand to bring new life to it
is that spiritual vigour within us that loves and longs for these words of God
a heart that sees, that loves the path and will follow willingly

faith is not an accessory, like a bag to hang on your arm
faith reaches out to the love of your life or nothing at all
this is the real sense of contentment in Jeremiah 29:13
you will seek me and find me when you seek me with all your heart.

have life and life everlasting
seek the Lord with all your heart

footnotes

1
Romans 5: 5
. . . and hope does not put us to shame,
because God's love has been poured into
our hearts through the Holy Spirit who has
been given to us

Pe

Psalm 119 : 129 - 136

Your testimonies
are wonderful

Pe

129
Your testimonies are wonderful;
therefore my soul keeps them.

130
The unfolding of your words gives light;
it imparts understanding to the simple.

131
I open my mouth and pant,
because I long for your commandments.

132
Turn to me and be gracious to me,
as is your way with those who love your name.

133
Keep steady my steps according to your promise,
and let no iniquity get dominion over me.

134
Redeem me from man's oppression,
that I may keep your precepts.

135
Make your face shine upon your servant,
and teach me your statutes.

136
My eyes shed streams of tears,
because people do not keep your law

shine on me

awe and wonder

doorway

border collie mode

three skylights

afterglow

awe and wonder

two opinions of God are here, one is you are wonderful I'm happy to obey
......the other is you are not wonderful and I will not obey
his own responses to those attitudes are awe in v129
and tears in v136 expressing emotional pain

we remember that God's words are a manifest of Himself
just as we express ourselves when we speak, our words reveal who we are and
what we are like
here God's expression of Himself in His statutes is described as 'wonderful'

our modern use of the word wonderful is somewhat devalued to become a pretty
adjective for example we say 'that's a wonderful cake''

'wonderful' when referring to God carries a sense of marvel
something incomprehensible, a miracle, wonder(ful) or full of wonder
as we see written in Exodus 15: 11

> "Who is like you, O Lord, among the gods?
> Who is like you, majestic in holiness,
> awesome in glorious deeds, doing wonders?

opinion, or what we think is invariably locked into a response, or what we do
we see it as people reveal their opinion of spiders by their response to them

the bond between the psalmist and God is wedded together in love
that his God is wonderful brings a sense of intimate delight and fellowship
happy to respond, to behave in accord   ....to obey

not surprising then in v136 his tears flow when his God is insulted by rejection
the rejection of our wonderful God is an insult to His name

as Jesus is maligned in our day as well
perhaps some tears would not go amiss

doorway

bi-fold doors are found in some places, uni-fold doors are everywhere
the word in v130 'unfolding' has a door as its root meaning
what is a solid wall can contain an opening to what is beyond

we are invited to see God's Word as a door standing open
a threshold for us to step over into His amazing presence
where He Himself will give light and understanding

this doorway opening event requires meekness
the word 'simple' here does not mean stupid
the idea implied is uncomplicated, perhaps receptive, not editorial

a person reading the Bible can be seen as acquiring understanding
just as we would unfold a package to discover its content
we call the Bible a living Word, a dynamic word with life embedded in it
but to the careless and untrusting it is a dead text

rewind vs129-130
we are seeing God's statutes are wonderful, elevated, and a marvel,
we hold this written Word in our hand with awe and wonder
in a way we imagine we are approaching God Himself
how heightened will our reading be with this in mind

border collie mode

vs131-132 lead us to another thought and reaction event
some of these events are commonplace - for we often 'look down our nose', or
'turn up our nose' in response to an internal sensation!

if we *open our mouth and pant* v131- what attitude are we conscious of?
perhaps the active eagerness that is reminiscent of a Border Collie sheepdog

the temperament of those particular dogs is listed as tenacious, intelligent, keen,
responsive, alert and energetic

so far   v129 Your words generate awe and wonder
           v130 Your words allow me through a doorway to understanding
           v131 my experience of Your words make me alert and attentive

seeing these words are true, would not awe and wonder follow
at the sight of such wonder who would not want to be part of it
a love of Him and His words would naturally follow

for an everyday suburbia .... that trilogy contains some high octane thinking
it's one thing to have religion, but religion like that may be a step too far
after all, who wants servitude or unreasonable expectations thrust on them

I have in my studio three skylights - over time they become dim with dirt and algae
- and the light is diminished
I then take a ladder, a broom and a bucket of soapy water to wash them
consequently the light is restored

turn to the beautiful v132 grace guaranteed to those who love Him!
let's get ourselves up and to that unfolding door
ready to welcome divine light and understanding
as well as a transformed temperament akin to a Border Collie

three skylights

when my skylights grew dreary, I moved into action
this module encourages us to ask and take action

skylight 1 v133 *let no iniquity get dominion over me*
steady my steps means please influence my inclinations to be aligned to the Bible
remember when we are out shopping, our feet naturally follow our will
here we are asking God - please configure my will (my likes) to be in accord with
the Bible (Your words)
do I really want God to start tweaking what I like
..... even when I know this will take me closer to Christ
do I want this window cleaned - do I want more light in this corner?

skylight 2 v134 *redeem me from man's oppression*
earlier we came across oppression, a violation of our person, a spiritual rape
when world thinking overrides and contaminates our inclination to Bible thinking
when we say 'I'll share my faith but not today', 'I'll pray later, not just now'
secular alternatives come in to violate our noble idea and we give in to them
do we really want to be delivered?

skylight 3 v135 *shine upon your servant*
and what does *make your face shine upon your servant* mean?
the couplet includes shine and teach
2 Corinthians helps by taking us back to creation[1]
when in those early days God's light illuminated the darkness

Christ can give us spiritual illumination now
we say, shine on me - as you lit up the world, please light up my mind
that is a very large scale illustration for us to take in

these three skylight prayers go deep, deeper than they first appear
they really test our integrity

afterglow

this module started with
the glow of the wonderful statutes (words) alongside personal accord v129
then concluded with
tears flowing in response to instances of that same Word being disregarded

a barometer is an instrument that is sensitive to barometric pressure ..... showing
sunny or wet according to a delicate mechanism within

all day long our sensitivity to Christ's person
is affected by accord, and it is affected by disregard
we are spiritual barometers in changing situations

speaking for myself as a barometer I'm lacking in the sensitivity department
I take great comfort in v132
turn to me and be gracious to me
as is your way with those who love your name

hear my prayers : please no sin - cleanse me from contamination - and shine love
and understanding on me
help tune my sensitivity

then .... we will also say your Word is wonderful
those doors will unfold for us to step into the presence of God Himself
and we will find a natural willingness to serve and obey

best place to be, ... wrapped up in Christ
do you want it,   pray the prayers

see things unfold

footnotes

1
2 Corinthians 4:6
For God, who said, "Let light shine out of darkness", has shone in our hearts to give the light of the knowledge of the glory of God in the face of Jesus Christ.

Tsadhe

Psalm 119 : 137 - 144

Righteous are you,
O Lord

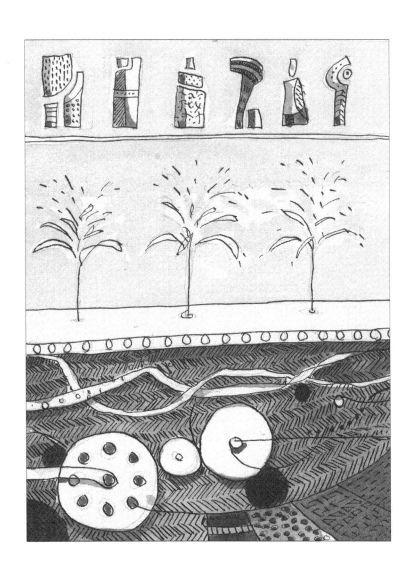

Tsadhe

137
Righteous are you, O Lord,
and right are your rules.

138
You have appointed your testimonies in righteousness
and in all faithfulness.

139
My zeal consumes me,
because my foes forget your words.

140
Your promise is well tried,
and your servant loves it.

141
I am small and despised,
yet I do not forget your precepts.

142
Your righteousness is righteous for ever,
and your law is true.

143
Trouble and anguish have found me out,
but your commandments are my delight.

144
Your testimonies are righteous for ever;
give me understanding that I may live.

springs of water

testimonial

all through the Psalm we have been guided through a progression of thought
now we are on a plateau of awareness that is foreign to the unbelieving world
here we challenge accepted formulas for living that are the norm in our society

in general the accepted formula is ....
a happy life will ensue when you get your lifestyle and personal environment right
this orchestration of various lifestyle choices will deliver a good life
how clever we are with our choices and how lucky we are with opportunities
which will prescribe how happy we will be

different people will make different choices, for some, an eco home in a Welsh
woodland, for others a sharp city apartment
we may be a lone entrepreneur or a corporate climber,   no matter
just discover what floats your boat - go for it and find happiness
one life, live it

Tsadhe champions an alternative view
lock on to these spiritual maxims ... that God is true and righteous
and find a completely different way of thinking
our man brings us a testimonial of the things he loves and bring him delight
what he has found in his relationship with God he shares with us

such an appreciation of God's maxims will recolour all previous priorities

sadly this way of life brought animosity and threats from those around him
he did not seek to change his circumstances but rather to understand them!

the basic principle

righteous and righteousness occur in vs137-138
the Hebrew letter of this module 'Tsahde' carries the meaning 'righteous'
the module celebrates the righteous person
God is righteous as defined in Deuteronomy 32:3-4[1]
this is not just a core rightness but an embodiment of **active** rightness

righteousness then is an active and visible outworking of inherent rightness
such statements are an affront to postmodern thinking where the consensus is that
no 'word' is actually true
words can only reflect an opinion to be translated
to a contemporary mind, these two verses present an outrageous proposition

nevertheless, this is his basic principle
a basic calculation fit to establish an entire life on
and this he confirms from a life of experience where he has found the calculation
to be entirely trustworthy v138

a living God who is active in righteousness
as opposed to idols or humanistic theories

Your words are right and they are living statutes
God himself lays out rightness in a series of statements v138
they are not only a description of Himself, they are part of Himself
a vital dynamic rightness suspended in this living, text

God and the Bible are a fountain of rightness that is to be our foundation
whatever people say

a diary of events

try to visualise here an experienced pilgrim reporting to his line manager with
vs139-141 as his comments

the core of the three verses is v140 where love and satisfaction are clearly the
top comment
everything in the basic principle has been thoroughly tested and found good
he, as the obedient servant is head over heels in love with the promises
they are given a five star review

the conditions in the field however were grim
that ardent love he had for the promises brought pain and problems v139
because the enemy Satan and the unbelieving world reject God's words
everything changes and nothing changes

for the word *small* in v141 read insignificant
he is *despised* - trodden on - regarded as nothing
in this he does not forget the basic principle

it was holding this set of maxims that brought on the problem
his ardent passionate love for the maxims now overrides any discomfort
he is sounding a bit like that other enthusiast, the apostle Paul[2]
he is not alone

let's audit our method for finding contentment and happiness in this life
do we prioritise the orchestration of our surroundings
or do we major on God's words and rise above the trials

conclusions

at the Palace of Versailles there are gardens and fountains on an immense scale
out of sight are massive valves that release water to those fountains
a good effort for a king, but God does big on a galactic scale
God's righteousness is a fountain of promises, provision, security and truth
'righteous' is not passive, it's dynamic
unlike a static pool, it's a fountain bursting with His righteousness

God and His words are everlasting and true
it's been tested as we saw in v140   and by Paul[2]
happily, for the child of God this experience is not reserved for the last day
not dreamy, one day over the rainbow stuff
this immense fountain of righteous joy is for now
Jesus spoke of *a spring of water welling up to eternal life* [3]

God's fountain will not dry up any time soon   it is everlasting
Versailles fountains only worked on occasions, due to limited supplies of water
with our God there is no limit, it's 'according to His grace' which is boundless
we will never be wanting
God's right is right, it's not an opinion or a translation
our God is truth

late in life David endured injustice, battles, insurrection and temptation
he said, in my time I've seen trouble and distress
but of no consequence when compared to the delight given by your commands
v143

he says
first embrace the Lord, feel and know life welling up in you
then look around at your circumstances

encore

we have adopted this French word for 'more of the same'
we see it's possible that the fountain of God's righteousness could well up in our
lives every day
observing David and Paul it may be an upgrade we would do well to emulate

it's like having a cute little cat and being offered a lion instead!
we say thanks but no thanks, we'll stick with cute

it would be awful though - if we were missing something
if in this one life we chose pathetic when super-abounding was turned down
is there a way for the cute christian to crank open valves of an enormous fountain
of righteousness

what does our man say?
give me understanding that I may live v144
it's a prayer
not any prayer, it's one we may have to persist with for a while
back to Jesus at the well, where He said 'ask and I will give you living water'
and then we will live

an artist once said I want to live like a poor man but with plenty of money
that resembles the lot of a believer
we have the fountain of righteousness and everything it brings
and for a while we may be lowly and despised

will you pray the prayer
give me understanding that I may live v144

footnotes

1

Deuteronomy 32 : 3-4
For I will proclaim the name of the Lord;
ascribe greatness to our God!
The Rock, his work is perfect, for all his
ways are justice.
A God of faithfulness and without iniquity,
just and upright is he.

2
Romans 8 : 35
Who shall separate us from the love of
Christ? Shall tribulation, or distress, or
persecution, or famine, or nakedness, or
danger, or sword?

3
John 4 : 10-15
Jesus answered her, "If you knew the gift
of God, and who it is that is saying to you,
'Give me a drink', you would have asked
him, and he would have given you living
water."The woman said to him, "Sir, you
have nothing to draw water with, and the
well is deep. Where do you get that living
water? Are you greater than our father
Jacob? He gave us the well and drank from
it himself, as did his sons and his livestock."
Jesus said to her, "Everyone who drinks
of this water will be thirsty again, but
whoever drinks of the water that I will give
him will never be thirsty again. The water
that I will give him will become in him a
spring of water welling up to eternal life."
The woman said to him, "Sir, give me this
water, so that I will not be thirsty or have
to come here to draw water."

happy in God

Qoph

Psalm 119 : 145 - 152

I rise
before dawn
and cry for help;
I hope in your words

Qoph

145
With my whole heart I cry; answer me, O Lord!
I will keep your statutes.

146
I call to you; save me,
that I may observe your testimonies.

147
I rise before dawn and cry for help;
I hope in your words.

148
My eyes are awake before the watches of the night,
that I may meditate on your promise.

149
Hear my voice according to your steadfast love;
O Lord, according to your justice give me life.

150
They draw near who persecute me with evil purpose;
they are far from your law.

151
But you are near, O Lord,
and all your commandments are true.

152
Long have I known from your testimonies
that you have founded them for ever.

spiritual deportment

harvesting the wind

wind in the sails

action within

the mechanism

eternal foundations

harvesting the wind

I have a book on the history of windmills and their beginnings in the 12th century
about these ancient mechanisms of renewable energy employed to harness the
wind's energy
shrewd people have studied the wind for centuries to great benefit

Qoph brings to us a principle of God working in our hearts and lives
a key part of that work is the Holy Spirit who is sometimes likened to the wind
and we are moved to work and glorify God with our labour

the module is divided into four parts

the working windmill usually had four sails, nowadays they have three
windmills are carefully sited and arranged to catch the wind
a likeness to us being ready for the Holy Spirit to move and work through us

when the wind turns the sails there is action within
there are sounds and movements, turning and grinding
the believer too feels motion within as the Spirit moves

the mill mechanism converts corn to flour
there are material benefits from the action
like the spiritual benefits to us in this life

the mill was secure on solid foundations
the flour was evidence that the wind came
God's foundations are solid and eternal

wind in the sails

windmills are enabled by wind
the millers plea would be 'send me wind then I can grind the corn'
alone he was unable to turn the large stones that ground the corn
vs145-146 about enablement alongside our limitations

as a child we were taught to say please and thank you as it was 'good manners'
'please' is not just politeness, it transforms 'give me' from a demand into a plea
pride interferes with prayer . . . . . . to make a plea is against the nature of pride

our prayers remind us of our needy status and that it is humbling to ask
it is true that we can be persuaded to say please against our will
but here *with my whole heart I cry* is not a pressurised statement v145
it reflects a sense that all bounty flows from the Lord
and that joy is embedded in a true relationship with God

a reminder that being together in everything is best
we have to be right in our thinking to receive anything from God
the miller turns his entire mill to catch the wind
every effort is put into making the windmill face the wind knowing that
otherwise it would remain lifeless

this enables the wind to turn the sails

humility enables God to pour His love into our hearts - and then we can and
will obey His laws
we know the Lord resists the proud and comes close to the humble[1]
humility is enabling

action within

getting things in motion
look at the movements in vs147-148
rising early, the cry of hope, eyes open and meditation   lots of spiritual activity
machinery in the windmill is active only when it faces the wind
the chocolate comes after please is said

deportment is another word for body language
how we hold ourselves reveals how we are thinking.
custom officers and the police are trained in this observational science
because our motives are naturally reflected in our deportment

it would appear this holds good in our spiritual life as well
our spiritual deportment can enable or prevent the motion of God's will
we can detect when people stiffen,
God can surely see us stiffen in our hearts, when pride kicks in

the millers task was to position the mill's sails
then the wind did the work and the mill stones turned
our work is about deportment
facing God in the right attitude - willing and wanting
then the work of obedience is easy

the care of our spiritual deportment needs continual attention
attitudes need to be audited

living for eternity - meditating on God's promises - saying prayers are transformed
spiritual things come to life when spiritual body language is right
humility is enabling

the mechanism

the wind blows and the wheels in the mill mesh together in harmony
they turn and interconnect according to the laws of engineering
words like accord, alignment, synchromesh indicate in harmony

we've called out to God with all our heart, this embodies humbling vs145-146
God responds to the humble , He says He gives grace to them[2]
we have become more animated in trust and meditation vs148-149

look at v149 for a poetic version of this harmony in the life in the believer
we can see the spiritual deportment of one who is asking for life and grace
hear my voice according to your steadfast love
O Lord, according to your justice give me life

Jesus reflects this thinking with His invitation in Matthew 11: 28-30
come to me, all you who are weary and burdened, and I will give you rest.
take my yoke upon you and learn from me
for I am gentle and humble in heart, and you will find rest for your souls
for my yoke is easy and my burden is light.

here law and love agree in confession, forgiveness and desire
in this intimacy our words harmonise with Christ's words
the wheels of faith and trust begin to turn

eternal foundations

there are people who have no inkling about God's law or what it calls for in
vs149-150
we can be so near and yet so far away

but You are near O Lord I have experienced it
I have learned about spiritual deportment - learned how to approach God
about what 'in accordance with your love' means to me
the intimacy of love - Song of Songs 2:14
> *O my dove, in the clefts of the rock, in the crannies of the cliff*
> *let me see your face, let me hear your voice*
> *for your voice is sweet, and your face is lovely*
here our Lord is speaking as a bridegroom and talking to us as a bride
this is nearness

the Almighty is terrible in His Holiness
but we are near Him when in accordance with His love
in the arms of His Son who gave himself for us on Calvary
His righteousness can be ours,
we can be wrapped in His robe of righteousness
nearness is safe

v152
not only now but for always
the poetry of *long have I known .... founded them for ever*
while human love is a fleeting thing, as long as life at best

Robert Burns famous love poem 'au fond kiss' is about parting
in contrast, our loving intimacy with Christ is for ever
there is no parting
let us set our sails turning, feel the Holy Spirit moving within us,
and hear His voice - near for always

footnotes

I
Luke I:51-53
He has shown strength with his arm;
he has scattered the proud in the thoughts
of their hearts;
he has brought down the mighty from
their thrones and exalted those of humble
estate;
he has filled the hungry with good things,
and the rich he has sent away empty.

2
James 4:6-7
Therefore it says, "God opposes the proud,
but gives grace to the humble." Submit
yourselves therefore to God. Resist the
devil, and he will flee from you. 8 Draw
near to God, and he will draw near to you.

Resh

Psalm 119 : 153 - 160

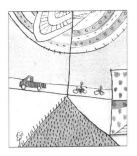

The sum
of your word is truth

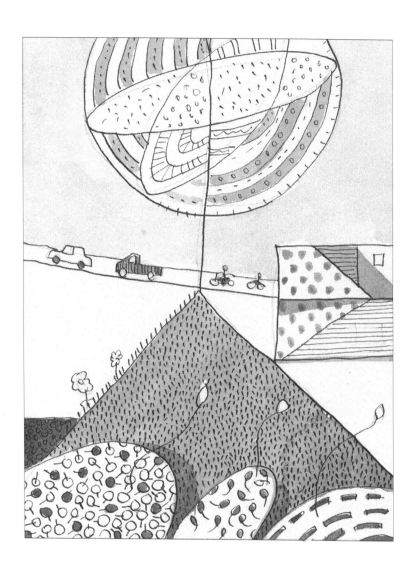

Resh

153
Look on my affliction and deliver me,
for I do not forget your law.

154
Plead my cause and redeem me;
give me life according to your promise!

155
Salvation is far from the wicked,
for they do not seek your statutes.

156
Great is your mercy, O Lord;
give me life according to your rules.

157
Many are my persecutors and my adversaries,
but I do not swerve from your testimonies.

158
I look at the faithless with disgust,
because they do not keep your commands.

159
Consider how I love your precepts!
Give me life according to your steadfast love.

160
The sum of your word is truth,
and every one of your righteous rules endures for ever.

drowsiness dispatched

perfect happiness

the essence

rumble strip I

rumble strip II

mutual love

perfect happiness

at the beginning of the Psalm our man saw happy, contented people
people who walked according to God's words and sought Him wholeheartedly
this had a huge effect on him
he said *O that I was steadfast* - like them

now, close to the end of the Psalm he writes Resh
he is steady in any situation like a gyroscope
doubt and anxiety are dispatched
there is a complete calm here, a contentment flowing from security written by a
steadfast hand

vs153-154 here is a realism and gyroscopic firmness
in life's inevitable turmoil God and His words are rock solid
my deep need finds a solution in God's provision of redemption

vs155-156 looks at a comparison of opposites that will refresh our conviction
our man sees that the wicked are not interested in God
while he asks for life according to God's rules

vs157-158 makes the comparison of unfaithfulness and steadfast love
those who prefer other loves are distasteful to him
he then uses recoil energy of emotion to work as an incentive to love

vs159-160 is where humility and God's steadfast love, connect
a fusion of His bounty and our need .... safety and security
living life according to love

the essence

this unit of thought rehearses relationship basics, the foundation of being
this four line snippet is packed with the essence of all 119 teaching
earlier in Zayin vs49-56 we noted the same thoughts in a formula for life
here it is again, with the sequence refreshed

1 experiencing this life v153
the relationship with God is working in the couplet - note the meeting of eyes
be looking at me and my situation, have your eyes on me and your arm to protect
I'll be looking, listening to Your words of law with eagerness as in v131

2 core foundations v154a
this is sounding so like the work of Christ we know about as NT believers
the way Christ works as our intercessor before a Holy God
made possible because of His work on the cross to bear the punishment for sin
in order to save us

3 knowing eternal reality v154b
this is life in the greatest sense, complete and eternal
give me life to escape this hostile environment, both NOW and ETERNALLY
God's promise here brings fellowship, unity, purpose and everlasting joy

on this solid and comprehensive base he moves forward with his observations
he is taking stock of things viewed from a position of strength
he is seeing this world from God's viewpoint, not seeing God from the world's
viewpoint

rumble strip 1

a huge contrast here v155
notice how swathes of humanity are not seeking out God's decrees
consequently salvation is light years away from them
he is highlighting this lack of interest and being intentionally provocative

why does he put this in the teaching manual now?
he is not one to make 'holier than thou' comments
on the contrary, he is sounding an alarm! a rumble strip to wake us up
this is designed to stir attention in the drowsy pilgrim
and on reflection I shiver at my own feeble attention to God's Word

immediately he provides the antidote, a diagnosis and the cure v156
suggesting we apply at once to God's compassion department
not in a token way but with serious intention
because a feeble spiritual pulse is very dangerous - take action

our Lord is big in compassion, He sees us coming as did the prodigal son's father[1]
He runs to meet us
He showers us with everything we need - when we get up and ask
think, where do we place our appetite for salvation on a scale of 1-10
then consider what number would trigger action

what is the prayer in v156, back in v154 and again in v159
give me life implies nurturing a precious thing in an aggressive environment
we certainly live in times of spiritual danger
which should reflect in our eagerness to pray

when we know the beauty of Christ and His saving power we will also know peace,
security and immense joy

rumble strip II

vs157-158 finds us looking at many active foes
again, not a statement of spiritual snobbery - 'I am better than they are'
it is more a review of our status to encourage determination
a recall of previous triumphs that we recorded earlier

negative external pressure can encourage strength
let's not read v157 like Eeyore from A A Milne in that melancholic attitude
this is a conqueror speaking - he has overcome - he did not turn aside
he will not swerve off the path, when the pressure is applied
not that he did it by himself .... rather God was working through him

we have two examples where the spiritual realm breaks into our awareness
v157 **persecution is felt** ... revealing our affinity with God
v158 **disgust is felt** ... revealing our affinity with God
these were evidences revealing the abstract spiritual world
and we saw demonstrations of faithfulness   *I do not swerve from your testimonies*
                                                                 the faithless .. do not keep your commands

earlier in v136 our man was in tears when God's words were ignored
here is a loathing of those who disobey and reject the Saviour

as a test for ourselves, how are we with blasphemy? OMG etc
does it pain us or are we immune to it
it's another rumble strip! it lets our known responses speak to us

our man is using comparison to generate life and spark attention to the path
there is a sense of joy at spiritual achievement v157
alongside sorrow due to the maligned Saviour v158

mutual love

God, out of kindness left us some rumble strips in His Word
they are manifestations of His costly love
He is saying, 'don't fall asleep, take care on the way'
places where we become cool: where spiritual drowsiness is a real danger
now He brings us close to Himself

vs159-160 where my humility and God's steadfast love connect
see 'I love' and 'Your love' come together in v159
where my faithfulness and love meets the steadfast love of the Redeemer
and life flows
as when our eyes met in v153
the thrill of feeling God's love in my heart is never forgotten once experienced

to be born again is to know that new life permeates our being
we say with thankfulness . . . all Your words are true . . . .and this is for eternity

remember the bridesmaids waiting for the groom Matthew 25[2]
drowsiness and neglect prevented entrance to the wedding
we live in dangerous times

but in the arms of the Saviour all is as it should be
life according to love, the wonderful steadfast love of Jesus

footnotes

1

Luke 15: 18-24

I will arise and go to my father, and I will say to him, "Father, I have sinned against heaven and before you. I am no longer worthy to be called your son. Treat me as one of your hired servants.'" And he arose and came to his father. But while he was still a long way off, his father saw him and felt compassion, and ran and embraced him and kissed him. And the son said to him, 'Father, I have sinned against heaven and before you. I am no longer worthy to be called your son.' But the father said to his servants, 'Bring quickly the best robe, and put it on him, and put a ring on his hand, and shoes on his feet. And bring the fattened calf and kill it, and let us eat and celebrate. For this my son was dead, and is alive again; he was lost, and is found.' And they began to celebrate.

2

Matthew 25: 1-13

"Then the kingdom of heaven will be like ten virgins who took their lamps and went to meet the bridegroom. Five of them were foolish, and five were wise. For when the foolish took their lamps, they took no oil with them, but the wise took flasks of oil with their lamps. As the bridegroom was delayed, they all became drowsy and slept. But at midnight there was a cry, 'Here is the bridegroom! Come out to meet him.' Then all those virgins rose and trimmed their lamps. And the foolish said to the wise, 'Give us some of your oil, for our lamps are going out.' But the wise answered, saying, 'Since there will not be enough for us and for you, go rather to the dealers and buy for yourselves.' And while they were going to buy, the bridegroom came, and those who were ready went in with him to the marriage feast, and the door was shut. Afterwards the other virgins came also, saying, 'Lord, lord, open to us.' But he answered, 'Truly, I say to you, I do not know you.' Watch therefore, for you know neither the day nor the hour.

Sin and Shin

Psalm 119 : 161 - 168

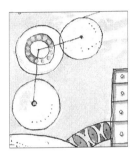

Great peace
have those who
love your law

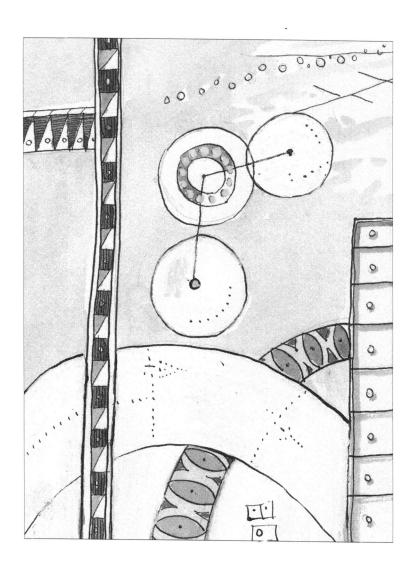

Sin and Shin

161
Princes persecute me without cause,
but my heart stands in awe of your words.

162
I rejoice at your word
like one who finds great spoil.

163
I hate and abhor falsehood,
but I love your law.

164
Seven times a day I praise you
for your righteous rules.

165
Great peace have those who love your law;
nothing can make them stumble.

166
hope for your salvation, O Lord,
and I do your commandments.

167
My soul keeps your testimonies;
I love them exceedingly.

168
I keep your precepts and testimonies,
for all my ways are before you.

great peace

outline

sin and shin are the same letter pronounced in a different way
the letter S sounding as 's' or 'sh'
it has nothing to do with our English words sin or shin

as the manual nears its conclusion, it rises to some quite sublime statements
the desire for the 'path' is increasingly synonymous with the writer's own objectives
the desire for steadfastness is becoming a reality

eight thoughts are presented in the eight verses
elements of life are interwoven with the living Word of God
the living Word in turn brings new vigour to those elements of life

I see them in three groups

observed dynamics vs161-163
he notes illustrations from secular life that serve to highlight his joy in God
pictures of persecution, warfare and falsehood are employed here

compound dynamics vs164-166
his daily activities are seen as vehicles for spiritual growth
a fusion of his deportment and the Spirit of God

intimate dynamics vs167-168
obedience merges with love and empathy
where great love for the person of God occurs
we recognise God's love filled interest in our ways

whoever finds this synergy desirable, to them it is not only possible, it's urgent

observed dynamics

energy and purpose abound in the secular world
the writer uses secular events to harness recoil energy to propel himself God-ward
not unlike when we have worked in a dirty shed, we long for a hot shower

v161 **persecuted without cause** or reason - a hollowness, a local emptiness
not so with Almighty God, every action backed up with reason
there is awe and respect for the words of the Almighty
..... by making the comparison he gets a sense of scale

v162 **the spoils of war** - rich rewards were claimed after winning the battle
historically there were processions by the victors displaying the spoils of war
in a greater way we relish God's benefits in hardship and conflict
rejoice with me the woman said to her friends and family when she found lost
treasure!

v163 **surrounded by falsehood** - as in our day where package overtakes content
after too much sweet food we long for some savoury
why sit moaning and whining in the midst of falsehood
when it could give us greater appetite for truth!

these three couplets do not exhaust the genre, they set us thinking
our era has much that sets our teeth on edge, that which makes us spit and tut
why not harness that recoil energy to propel ourselves nearer to God
and there refresh ourselves in the purity of God's promises and delight of His laws

compound dynamics

moving on from social realities that were observed and experienced
the next three couplets take a look at his private life
an observation of how he ordered his own time and attention
looking at David's life elsewhere we do not see him as austere, stiff or sombre
he entered into everything he did with all his heart, he was what we call 'full on'

these three couplets are 'full on' enjoyment
      - certainly not a tedious monochromatic exercise yard for sinners

v164 the number seven signifies **completeness**
praise and worship complete his days, his life
this may not refer to regular 'devotions' within a monastic timetable
praise cannot be commanded, it wells up from within, it is unstoppable
God's righteous laws are a joy as they regulate his days
his life and God's laws fuse into a compound

v165 peace within, still persecuted, but **great peace within**
this is flowing from love, not love dragged out of his own meagre store
God's love poured into the everyday, an overflowing of His abundant love
here is a compound that is unassailable - solid and not given to stumbling

v166 to hope in God is **a certainty**
looking for salvation in the Lord will not disappoint
when we have eyes to see our feebleness and the Lord's fullness things change
happy for His fullness to fill our emptiness and to see life changed forever
knowing that we are His and He is ours is the best dynamic ever

now what he feels for God will order what he does
because just doing things may not make you feel anything for God

intimate dynamics

now we are ushered into the intimate place
where willingness is unfettered, where love obeys with joy
there are no secrets here, all is known and shared

v167 is the confirmation of the sequence, **because I love I obey**
first on the scene was God who made us beautifully
then we in Adam were rebellious and fell into sin
the Levitical law had the sinner placing his hands on the head of the
animal sacrifice that would be a substitute for him
a tactile identification with the one who stood in his place
an intimate moment of connection
later Christ Himself came to be an atoning sacrifice to redeem us
an intimate moment of connection where we identify with the One who stood
in our place as an atoning sacrifice
His physical death was dreadful
bearing the wrath of God's judgement for my sin was so much more dreadful
this is love . . . . that God sent His Son . . . .with love and willingness

v168 is never a 'spy in the sky' statement
this is **the utter relief of complete transparency** - no anxious secrets remain
an intimacy that is complete
such Love - that knows all my ways - and loves me with a steadfast love
our only response is to embrace every aspect of our Lord

applied dynamics

I have called them dynamics because of the inherent energy in the statements

going to church is to engage in a formal meeting with God
we have many other informal opportunities to meet and commune with God
these engagements are part of our 'spiritual life'

if you wanted to, you could take a moment to review the vibrancy of this life,
to judge the measure and flavour of that interface between you and God
how lively, how dynamic is the connection between you and your Maker

we have viewed some beautiful benchmark 'fellowship with God' statements
eight couplets that fizz with life and love
I for one am awed by them
and noted that those who love Your law have great peace

nothing stands in our way of knowing that peace and joy
age, health, gender, intellect, status or colour are of no consequence
can we kneel though?
does our need of a redeemer melt our hard hearts?

we can rejoice in His promises, like one who finds great treasure
we can fizz with life and love
great peace can be ours, when we know the love of God in our hearts

footnotes

1
Luke 15:9
And when she has found it, she calls
together her friends and neighbours,
saying, 'Rejoice with me, for I have found
the coin that I had lost.'

Taw

Psalm 119 : 169 - 176

Let my soul live
and praise you

Taw

169
Let my cry come before you, O Lord;
give me understanding according to your word!

170
Let my plea come before you;
deliver me according to your word.

171
My lips will pour forth praise,
for you teach me your statutes.

172
My tongue will sing of your word,
for all your commandments are right.

173
Let your hand be ready to help me,
for I have chosen your precepts.

174
I long for your salvation, O Lord,
and your law is my delight.

175
Let my soul live and praise you,
and let your rules help me.

176
I have gone astray like a lost sheep; seek your servant,
for I do not forget your commandments.

carried home

happy anticipation

on calling and urging

the need for nurture

excited about life

carry me home

happy anticipation

returning home from London I use Victoria Station
this city rail terminal is a busy place where everyone is eager to be moving on to
their chosen destinations

Taw is a bit like that
a similar feeling of a journey, live departure boards and travel destinations
where we are checking possessions, platforms, times and tickets
and then falling into a moquette covered seat ready to move off

vs169-172 **on calling and urging**
ticking all the boxes, currency, visas and letters of introduction
the relief that we are not alone and God is with us
we acknowledge this with a prayer as we would text a friend

v173 **the need for nurture**
the train is welcome but I'm not home yet, many a slip between cup and lip
we do a visual check that the phone charge level is OK
if calamity occurs I'm not alone

vs174-175 **excited about life**
we close our eyes and imagine our destination being everything it should be
we long to just be there, to be united
transported back to how we felt when we were first in love

v176 **carry me home**
we've been away, we are still far away, now sitting helpless in a moquette seat
then the train begins to glide out of the platform taking you home
while you are still motionless in a moquette seat

on calling and urging

vs169-172 four pleas, cries or humble requests
expressed in an environment of God's free and abounding grace
they are distillation of a genuine awareness of need
two ask for provisions from God and two ask for ability to worship

voiced here is an acute awareness of things we ourselves are unable to furnish
(understanding and salvation)
as well as an acute awareness of abilities we ourselves are unable to furnish
(praise and worship)
and thankfully an awareness of where to apply . . . . .God Himself

there is a reality here - an urgency that is attached to responsibility
on the journey - ticking all the boxes, currency, visas and letters of introduction

v169 help me to understand what is going on!
                    where I need to be and what I need to have
v170 naturally I'm bound in sin, release me
                    I cannot release myself
v171 fill me to overflowing with praise
                    there is a danger of being full of myself - change this
v172 fill me with joy so I cannot help but sing

our man has experienced these four things before
when they work in concert within him he knows purpose, and joy
he is clear that they are not manufactured by himself - they are promised and
supplied by his Lord
all is from You; MAY it continue to flow

this is that perfect spiritual deportment
rejoicing in grace
everything in place
alongside relief, in the glow of a warm benefactor

the need for nurture

mind the gap, gentle correctives

the atmosphere of Taw is abounding love and trustworthiness
a sequence of continual positives,
recognising a rich bounty in its unshakable truth
that God and His words are valid currency in our day

while he is beside himself with joy in this relationship of trust and love
he knows himself to be the weak link in it

grace can be construed as feudalism in that medieval downtrodden sense
that we are crushed sinners grovelling with the occasional spiritual turnip
thrown to us

a far cry from the language of delight in Taw
there are clear pictures of love woven into its words
my plea v170, my lips v171, my tongue v172 and now His loving hand is requested
always ready, attentive to any wobble on my part
Lord, you are streaming good things to me continually
                                        in my weakness support me in Your arms
You are my choice, I choose You from my experience of Your Word

in our first verse he asks for understanding - because pride goes before a fall
knowing his weakness to pride he asks His Lord to be on hand - just in case

v173 feeds on the spiritual provisions in God's words that nurture him along
with a hand poised ready to support
we do a visual check that the phone charge level is OK
if calamity occurs I'm not alone

excited about life

until now it's been about establishing practicalities,
a list of parts and purposes laid out
today we can look back over his list and make a note of how we compare
do we recognise his spiritual deportment, his understanding of scale and status

it is a surprising list
it remains simplicity itself, with no intellectual levels to achieve, no academic
requirements, no cultural preferences
this genuine expectation of life eternal in Christ is open to all without exception
providing we kneel at the cross of Christ and confess our need of a Saviour
the thief on the cross demonstrates this truth to all

vs174-145 enters into the feeling and sensation of a sinner who has found a Saviour

we rejoice in the promise of salvation, of sins forgiven
we long for the realisation of that promise that is in glory
we close our eyes and imagine our destination, being everything it should be
we long to just be there, to be united

wrapped up in the Lord and His Word is a longing that is love, a delight and a
spiritual sustenance
food disperses into our body to maintain life and energy
as does the Lord and His Word to maintain spiritual life and energy

when so enraptured with this reality
our purpose of living will be praise

carry me home

T S Eliot wrote 'The Hollow Men', a poem that finishes with
this is the way the world ends, not with a bang but a whimper
'not' an expected ending
he was asked would he like to revise it, and on reflection, he said 'no'

David too surprises us with his last line, his going out with a whimper
at the end of the Psalm so full of the path to the joy of life eternal
he says he is like a lost sheep, I'm helpless, come and find me

this though **is the triumph of the Psalm,** when he comes to the end of himself
for the lust of the eye and the pride of life is our biggest enemy
in this last verse he records a victory over the insurgent self

throughout the Psalm requests abound 'may You do this, please give me that'
he knows His Lord must do all, while he kneels and praises
his greatest joy is to be a vessel , a container filled with his Lord

as Jesus himself said, *whoever finds his life will lose it, and whoever loses his life for my
sake will find it.* Matthew 10:39

along with this parable
Then Jesus told them this parable: *"What man of you, having a hundred sheep, if he
has lost one of them, does not leave the ninety-nine in the open country, and go after
the one that is lost, until he finds it? And when he has found it, he lays it on his shoulders,
rejoicing. And when he comes home, he calls together his friends and his neighbours,
saying to them, 'Rejoice with me, for I have found my sheep that was lost.' Just so, I tell
you, there will be more joy in heaven over one sinner who repents than over ninety-nine
righteous persons who need no repentance.*
Luke 15: 3-7

here comes the Lord, what a beautiful way to end - you and I being gathered up in
the arms of the Lord and carried home to rejoice with Him for always

23486531R00143

Printed in Poland
by Amazon Fulfillment
Poland Sp. z o.o., Wrocław